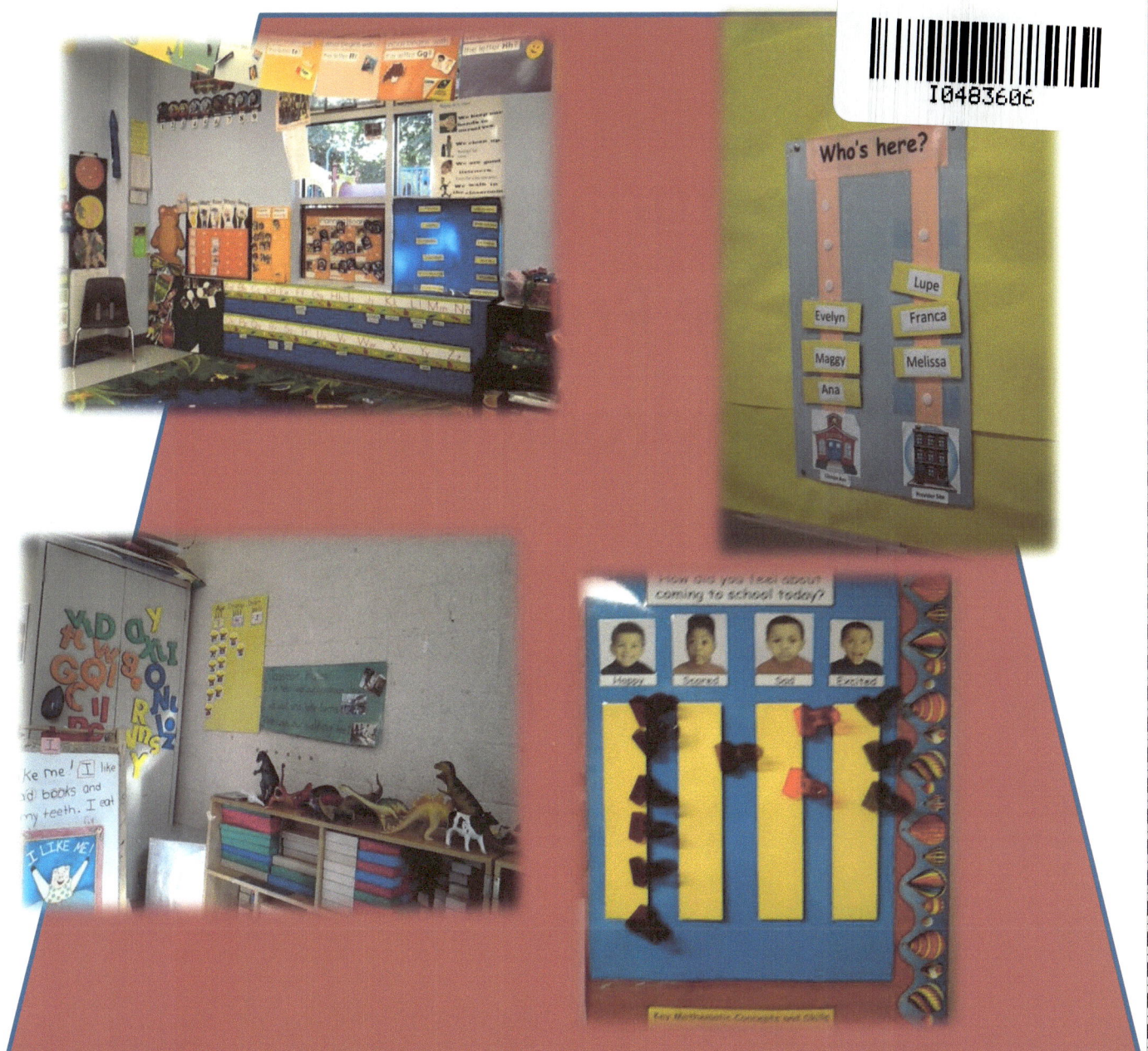

I0483606

A PICTORIAL REVIEW OF THE PRESCHOOL ENVIRONMENT

By Evelyn Ayum

"A Pictorial Review of the Preschool Environment"

By

Evelyn Ayum

Library of Congress Copyright 8/13/2016
Copyright #8-368-663
All rights reserved to Evelyn Ayum
No parts of this book can be duplicated, digitally, audio by no means without the author's approval.
First publication date November 30th, 2016
ISBN 13: 978-0966590180

This book was written as a resource for all teachers who need support with visuals for daily routine charts such as: job helper, attendance, linear calendar, weather and other useful charts—like the one below. In addition, there are other visuals in this book to guide teachers and support with the preschool environment. "A Pictorial Review of the Preschool Environment" is also a growing project and will constantly change and update as I compile pictures appropriately for the preschool classroom. I hope that you will use the book to support, what you do as a teacher in the preschool classroom.

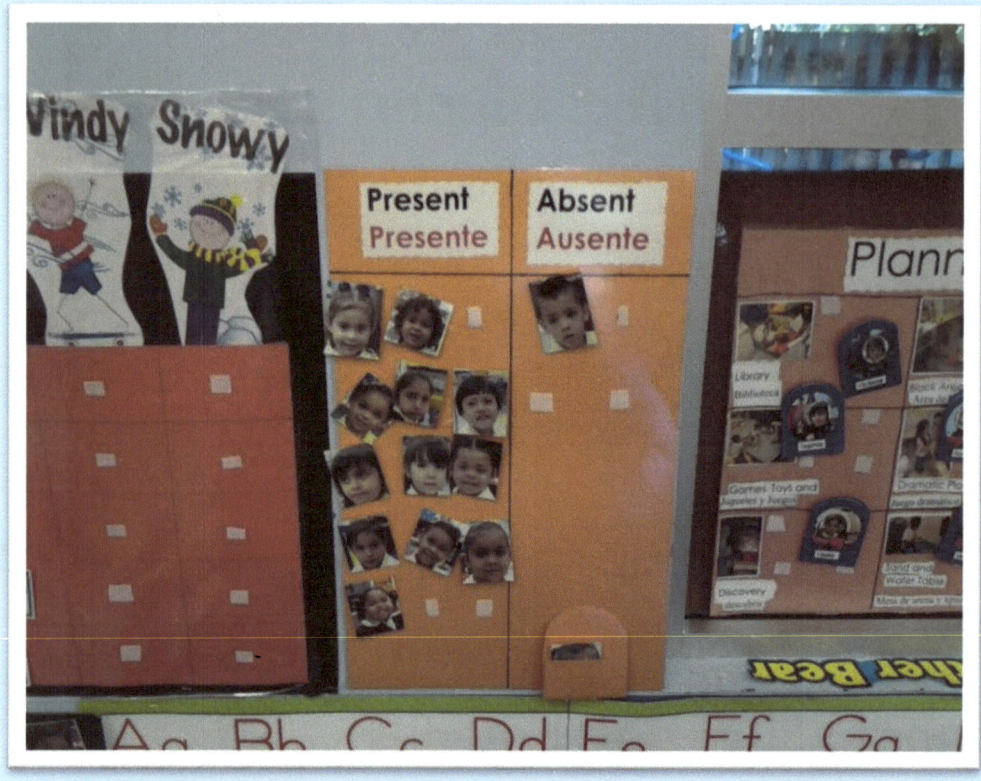

Attendance chart

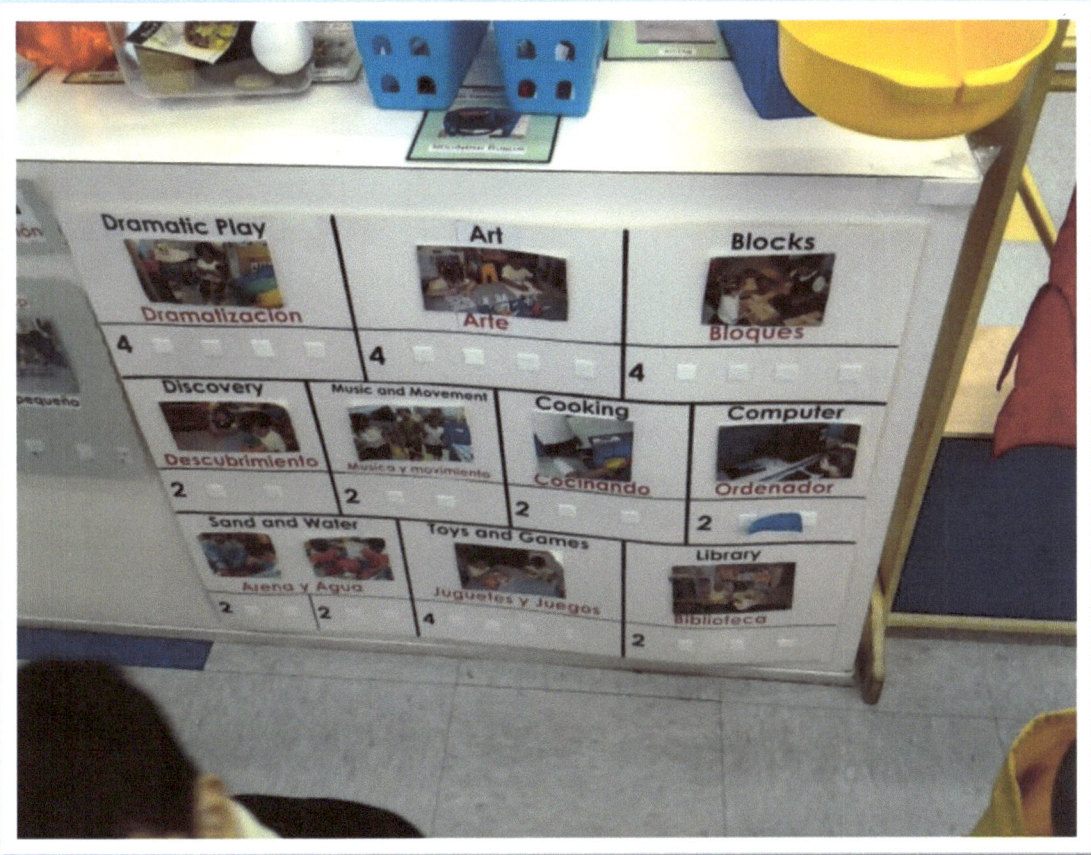

Planning board

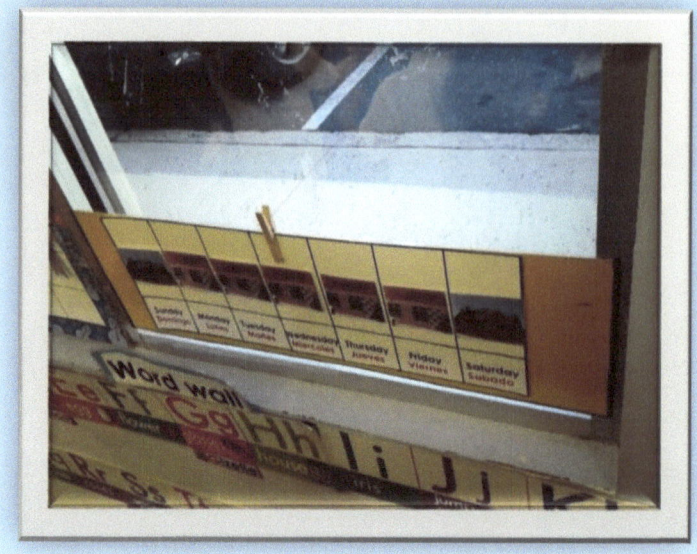

Linear calendar

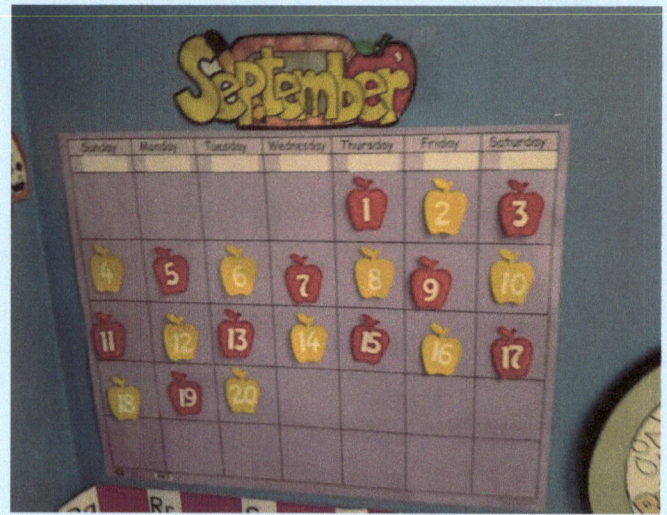

Calendar for older children

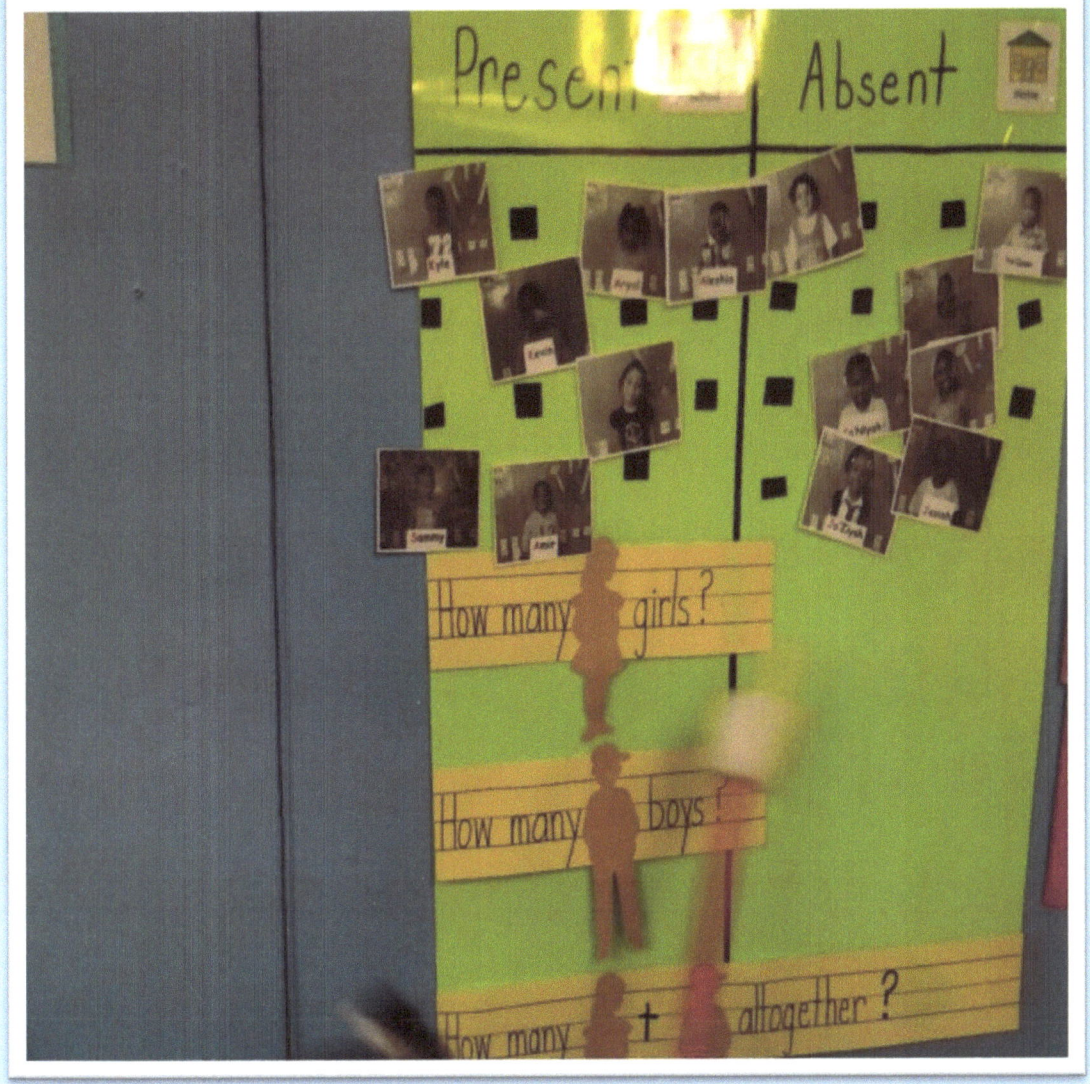

Attendance Chart

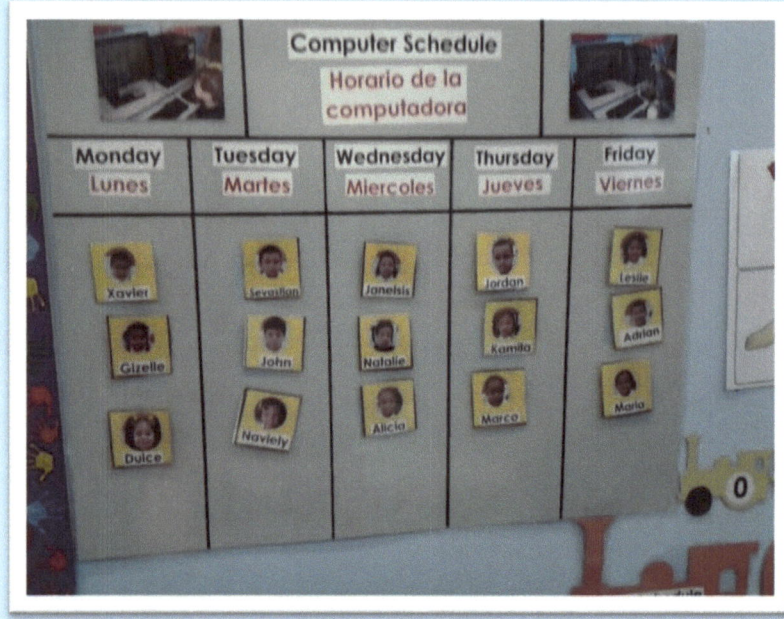

Schedule for the computer

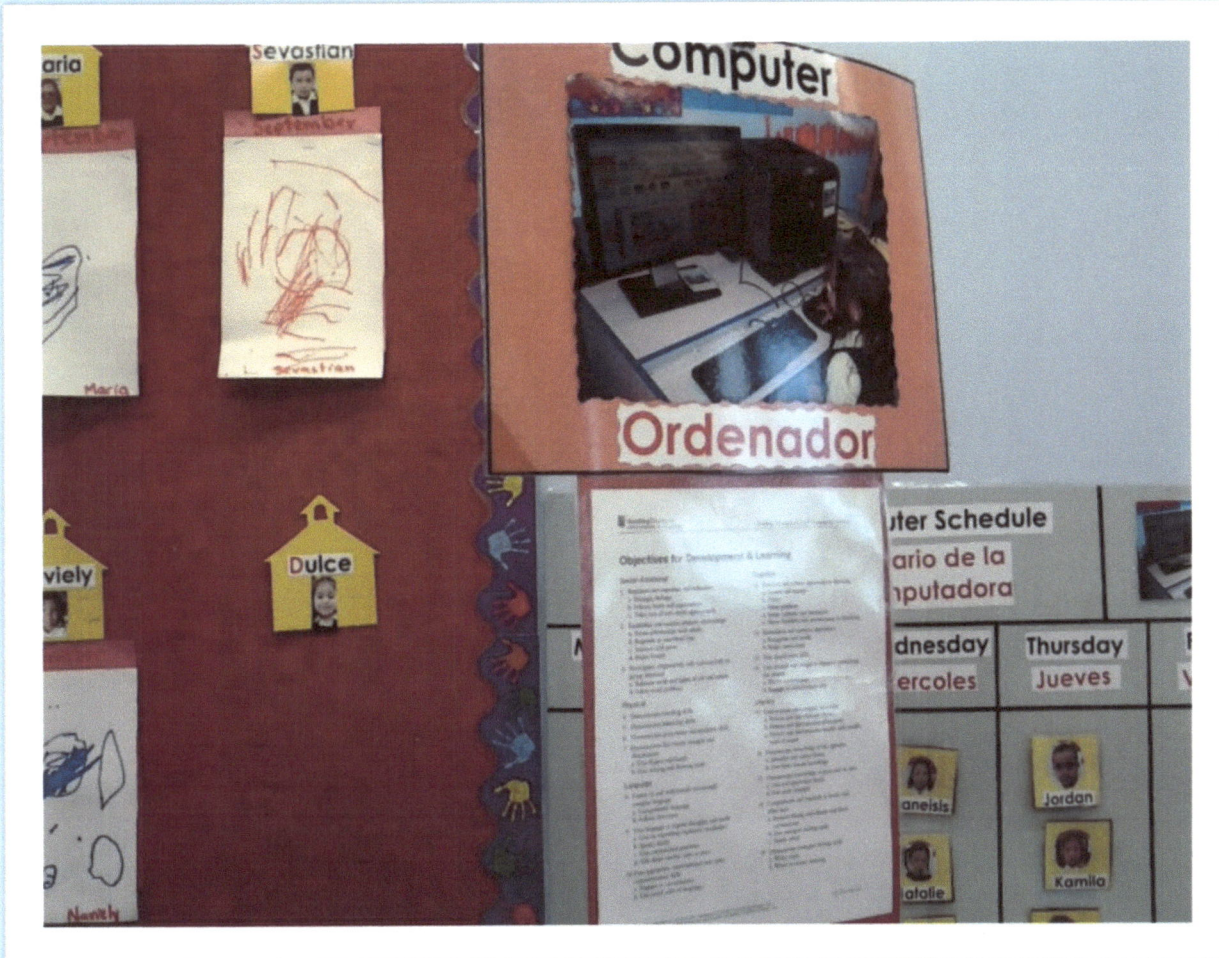

Computer schedule

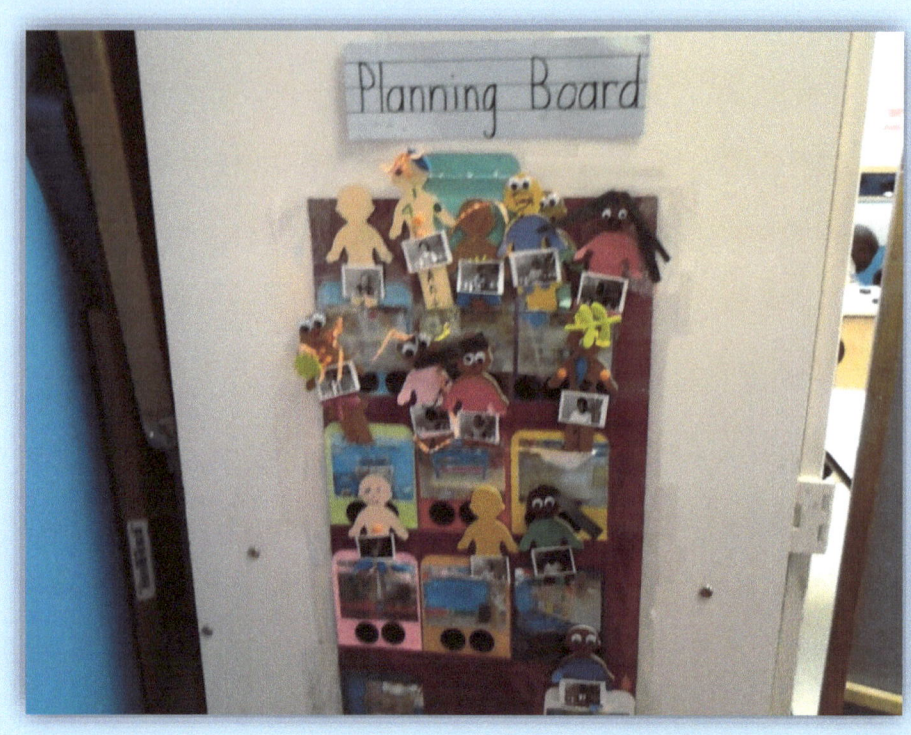

Popsicle sticks were used of children's faces so they can pick what interest area to play in.

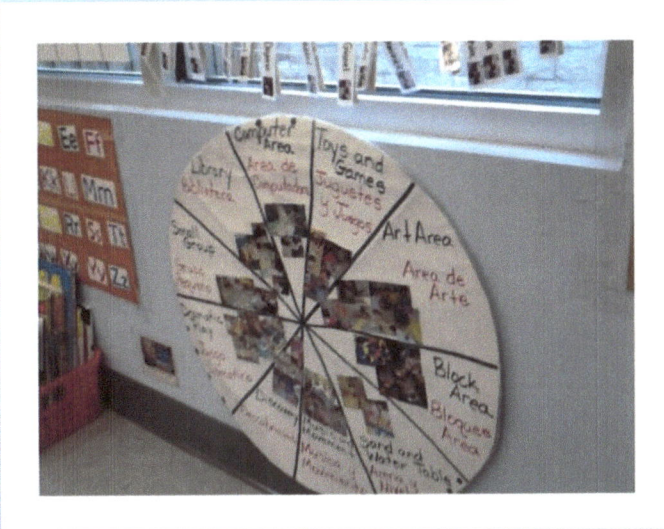

Planning board wheel used when lacking space.

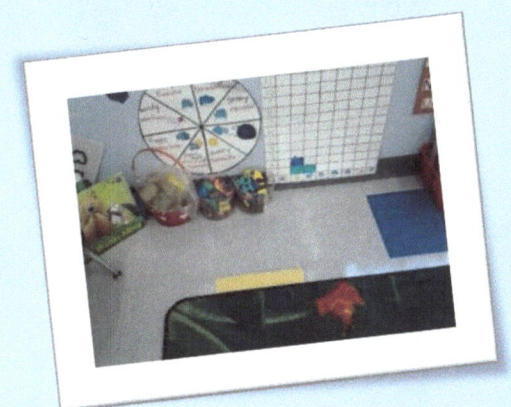

Weather Wheel

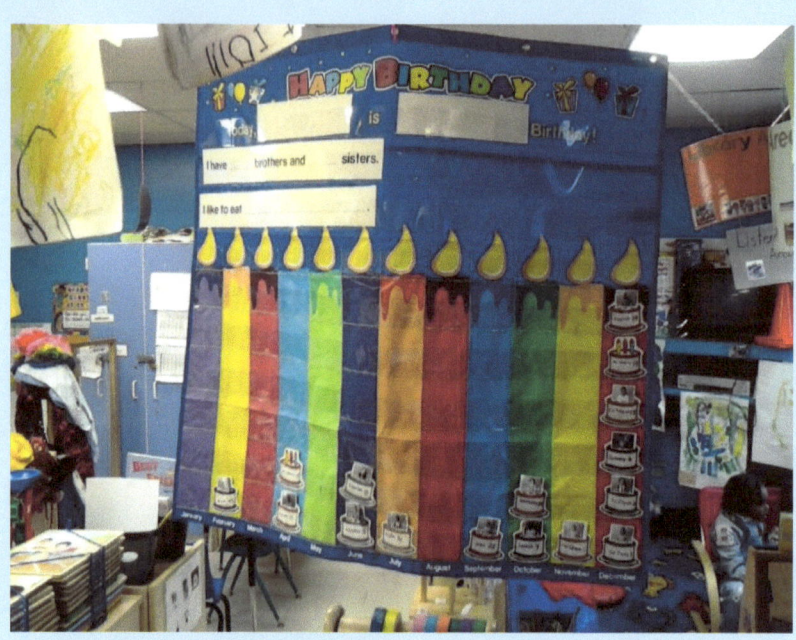

Birthday Graph

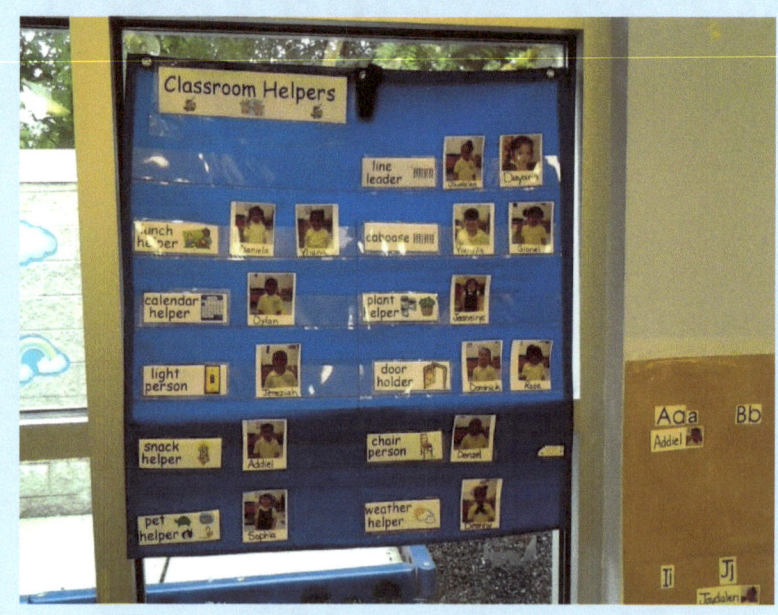

Helper chart

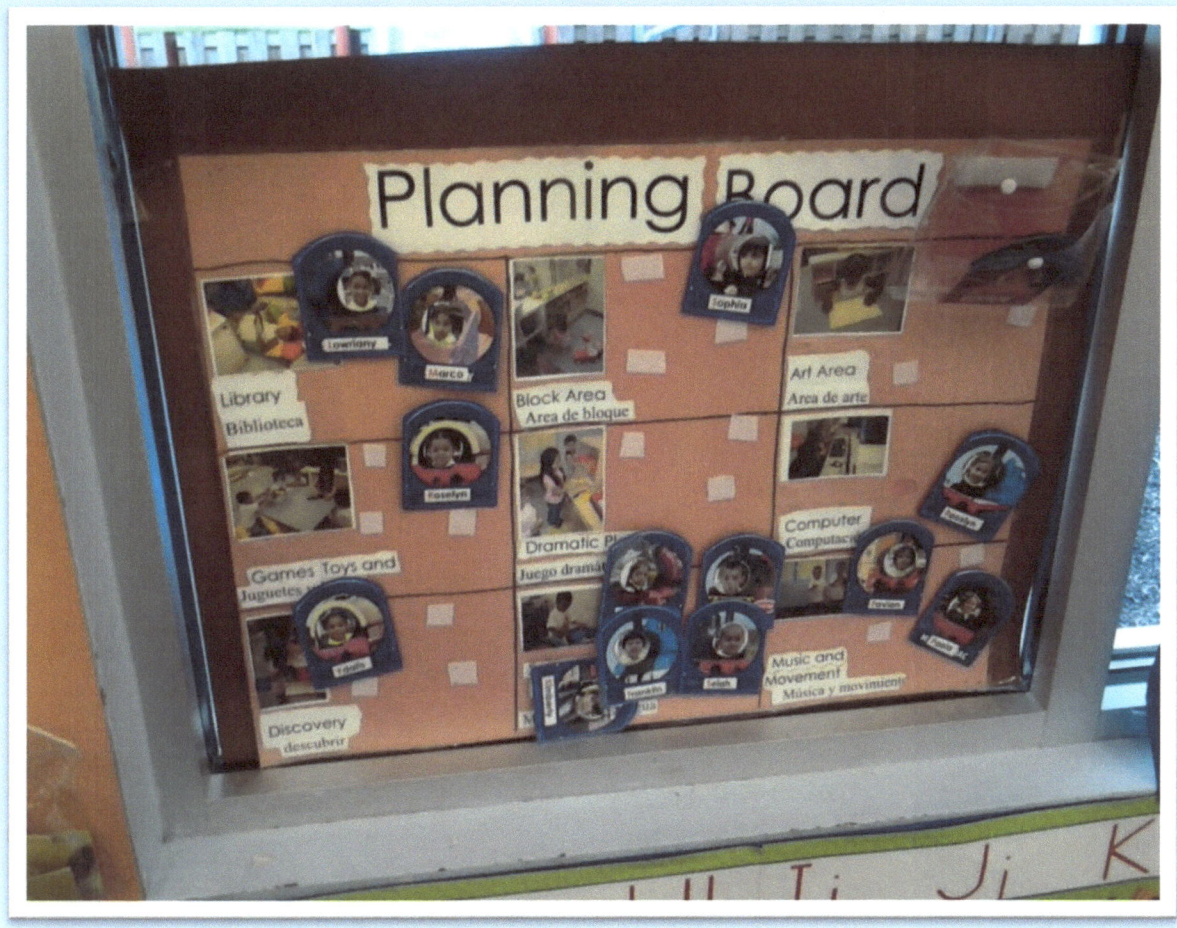

Planning board

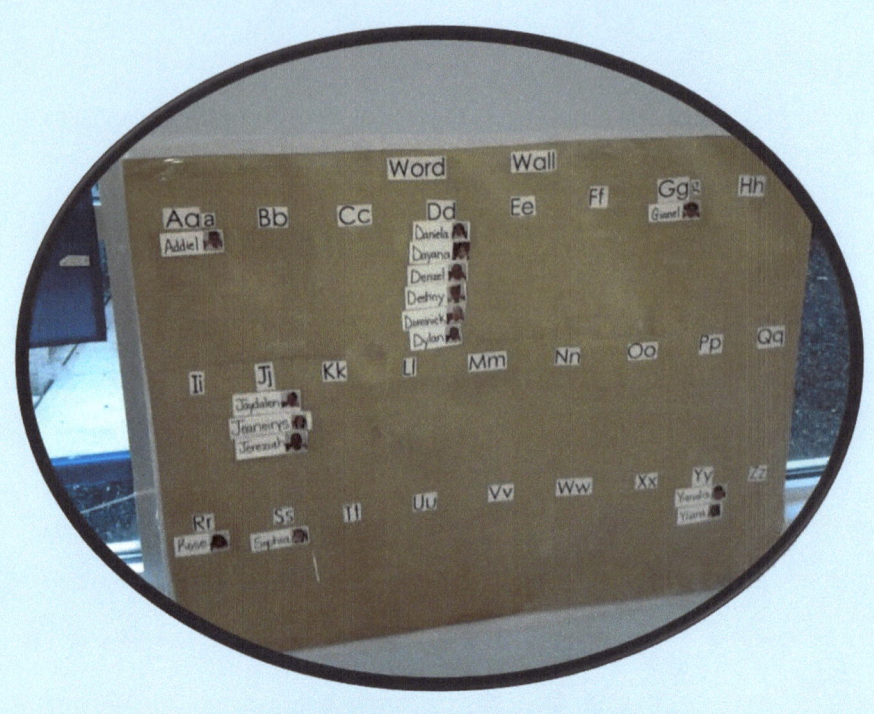

Word wall created using butcher paper as the background.

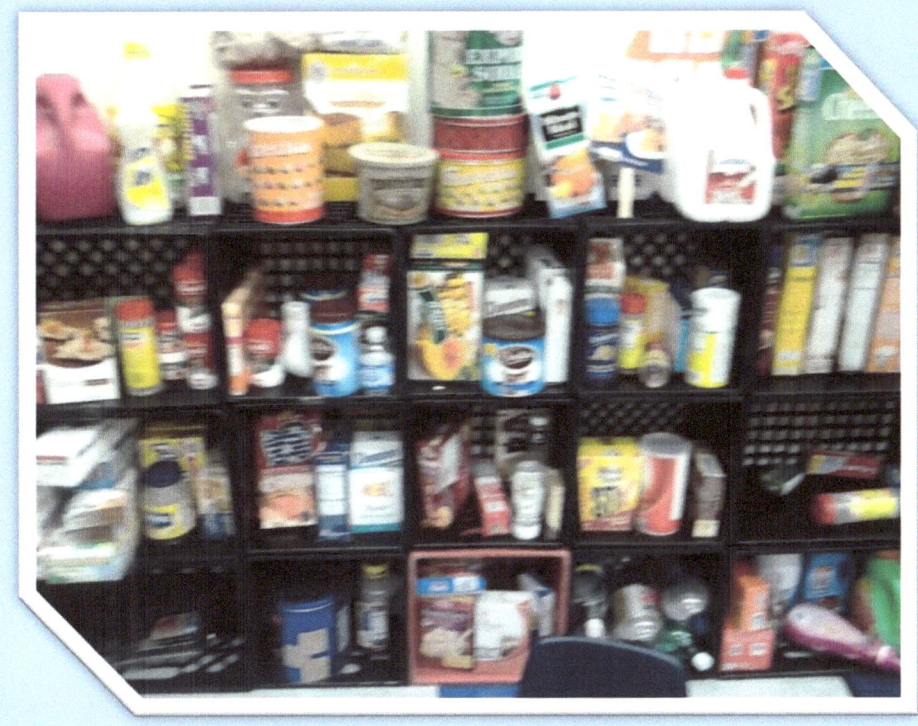

Grocery items in the dramatic play area can enhance environmental print for children.

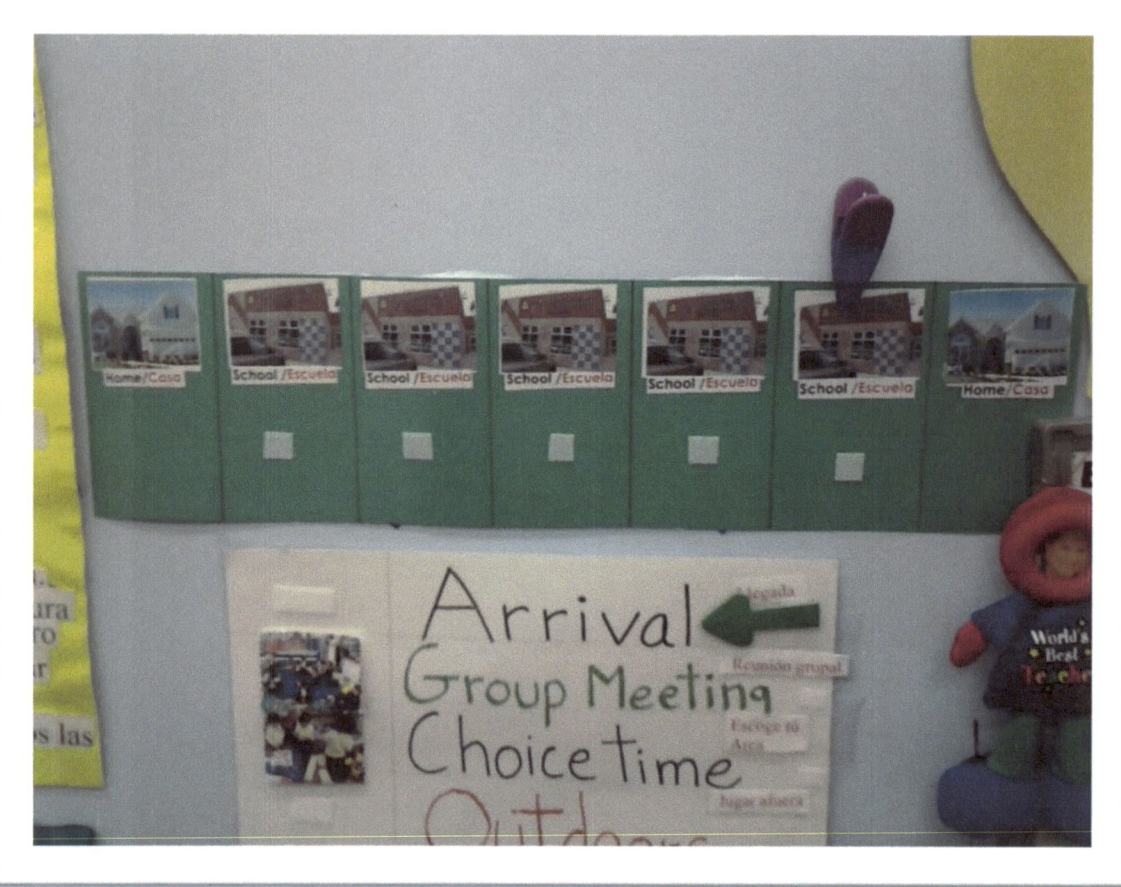

Linear calendar for younger preschoolers as an interactive activity.

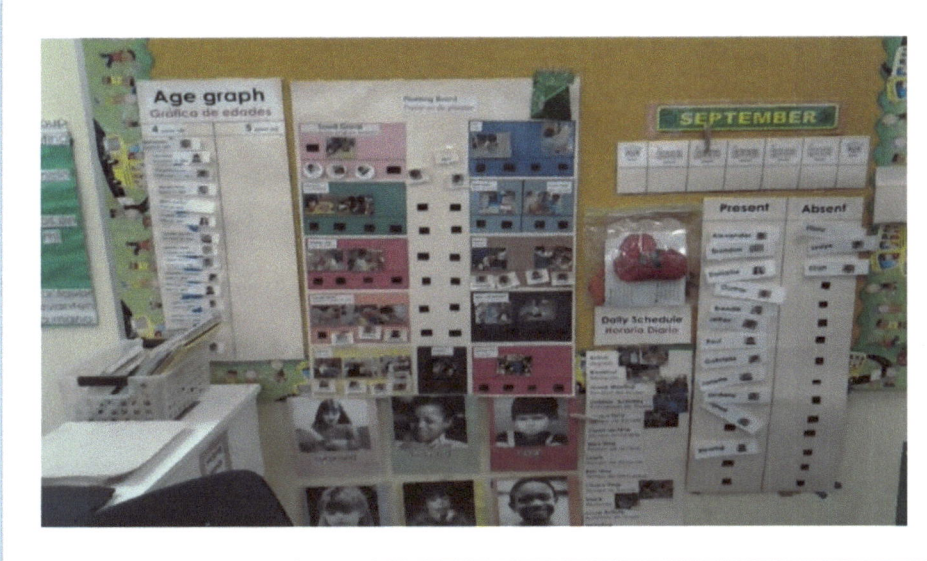

These are multiple posters for a room very little wall space. (Age graph, feelings chart, planning board, calendar and attendance chart). Look how the space is used.

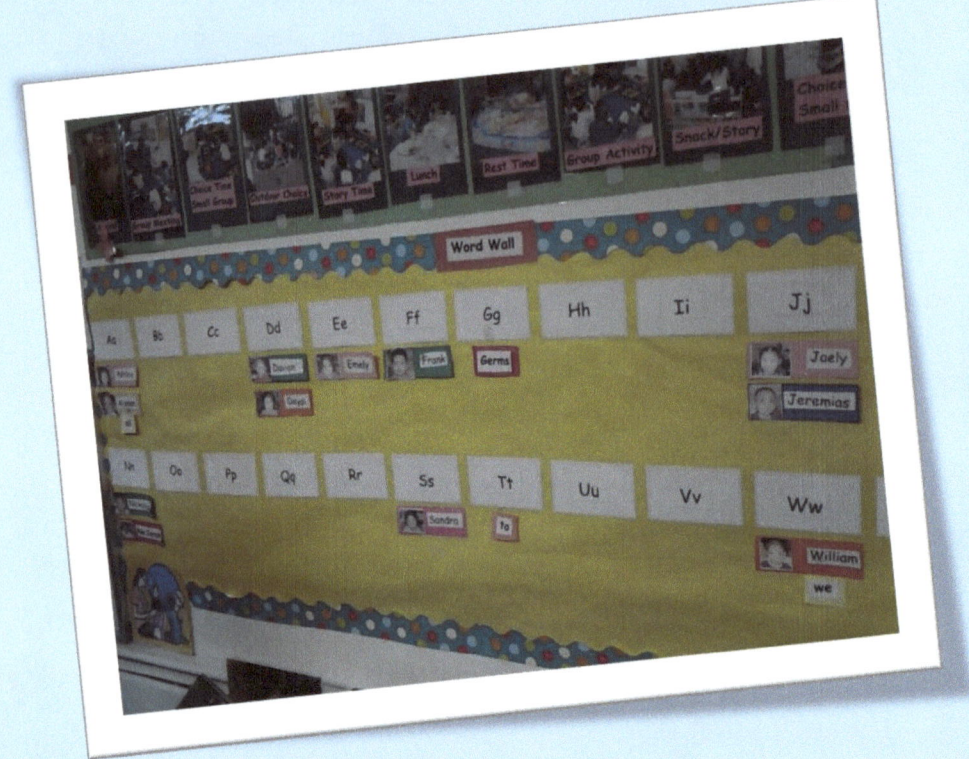

Here is an example of a preschool word wall and children's schedule above.

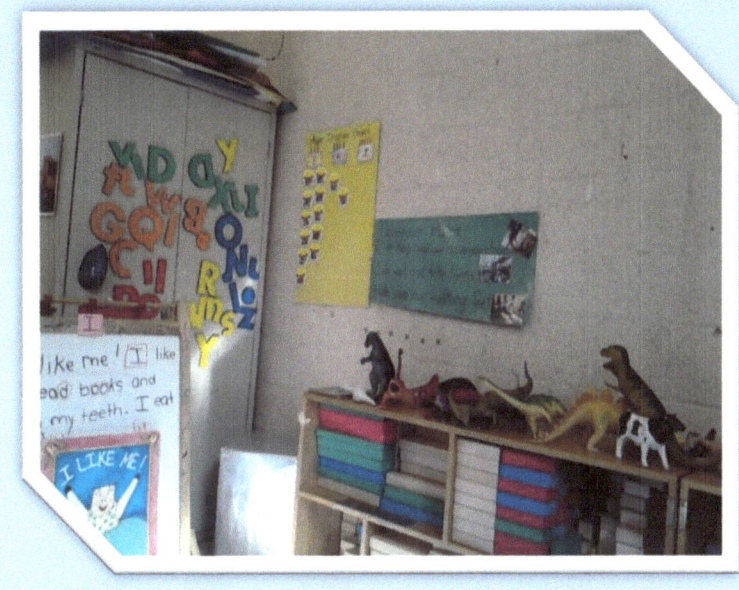

Notice how print is used in the block area. Plastic letters were used so children can manipulate. Ask children to tell about their building in the block area.

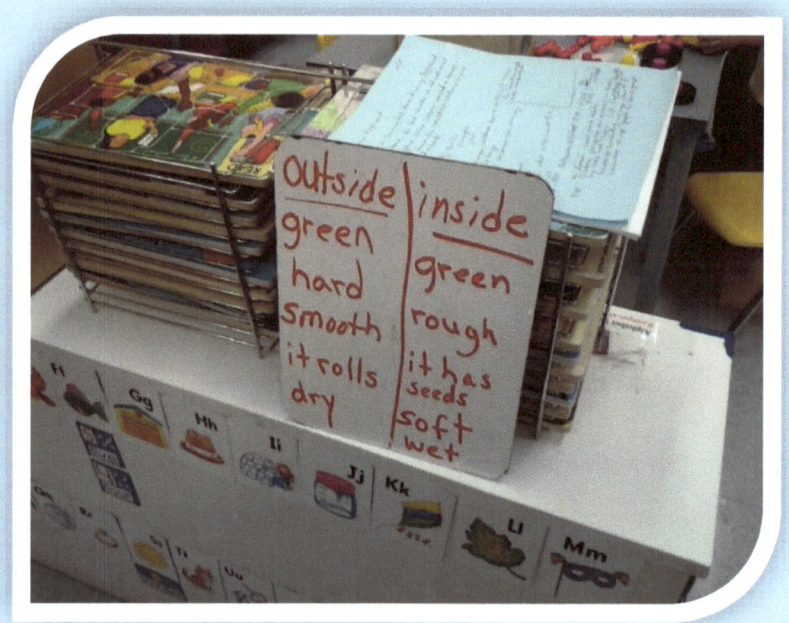

Documented here is what preschoolers learned about seeds. The whiteboard is used to show children that what they say can be written down.

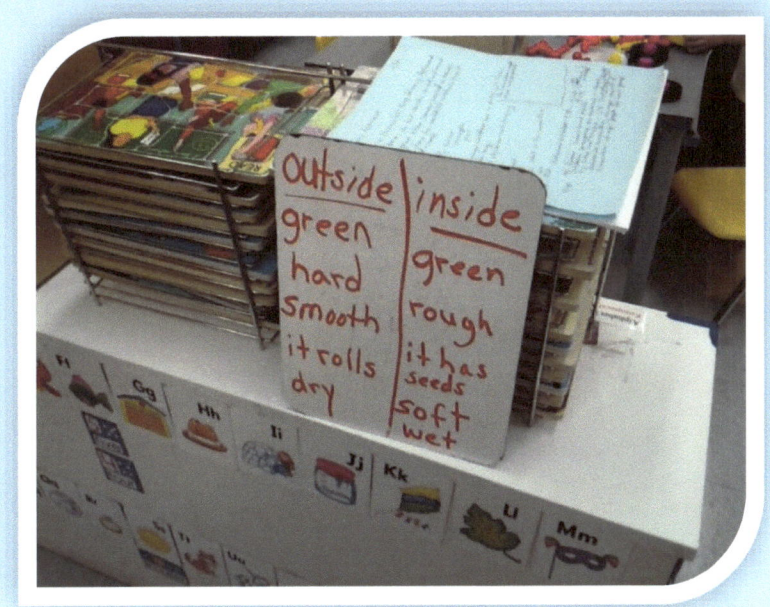

Add the children's name to what he/she said to demonstrate value to what was said.

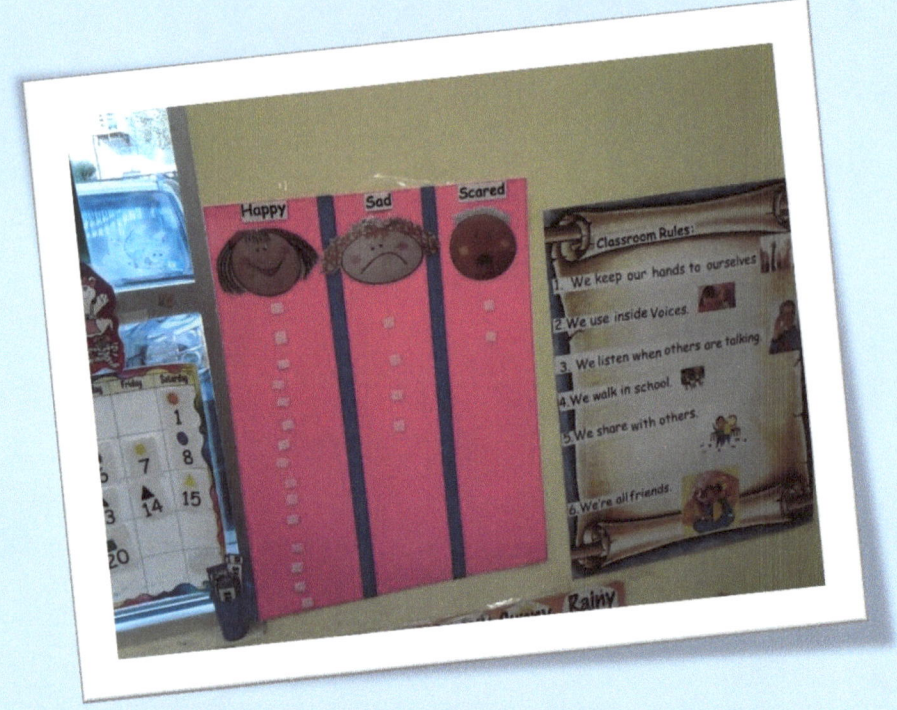

A feelings poster is used here so children can post how they feel. Think about how you can use writing to support in this area.

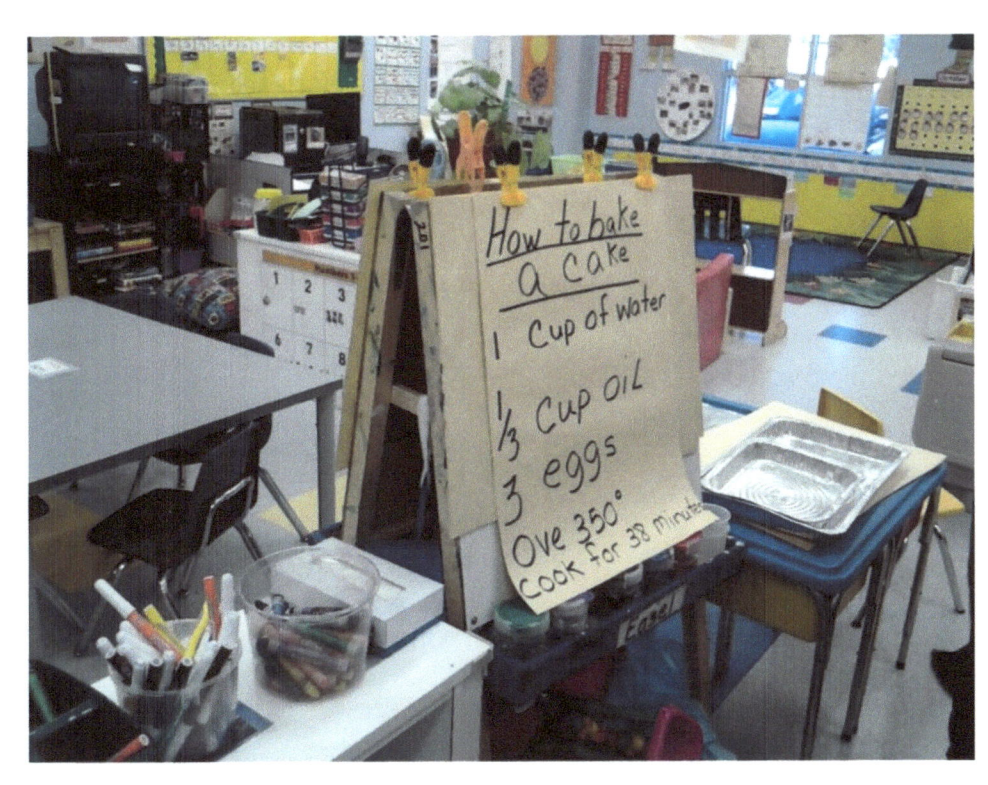

A recipe with words, what is missing from this cake recipe? Yes, use visuals to address all learners.

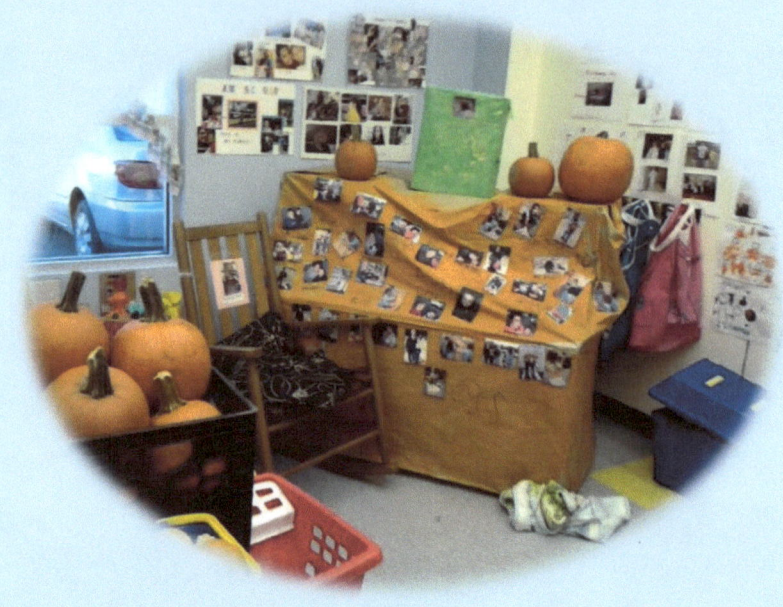

This is a great idea to "scream" the theme in the dramatic play area about the season. You still need to maintain the dress up clothing and make the kitchen items available.

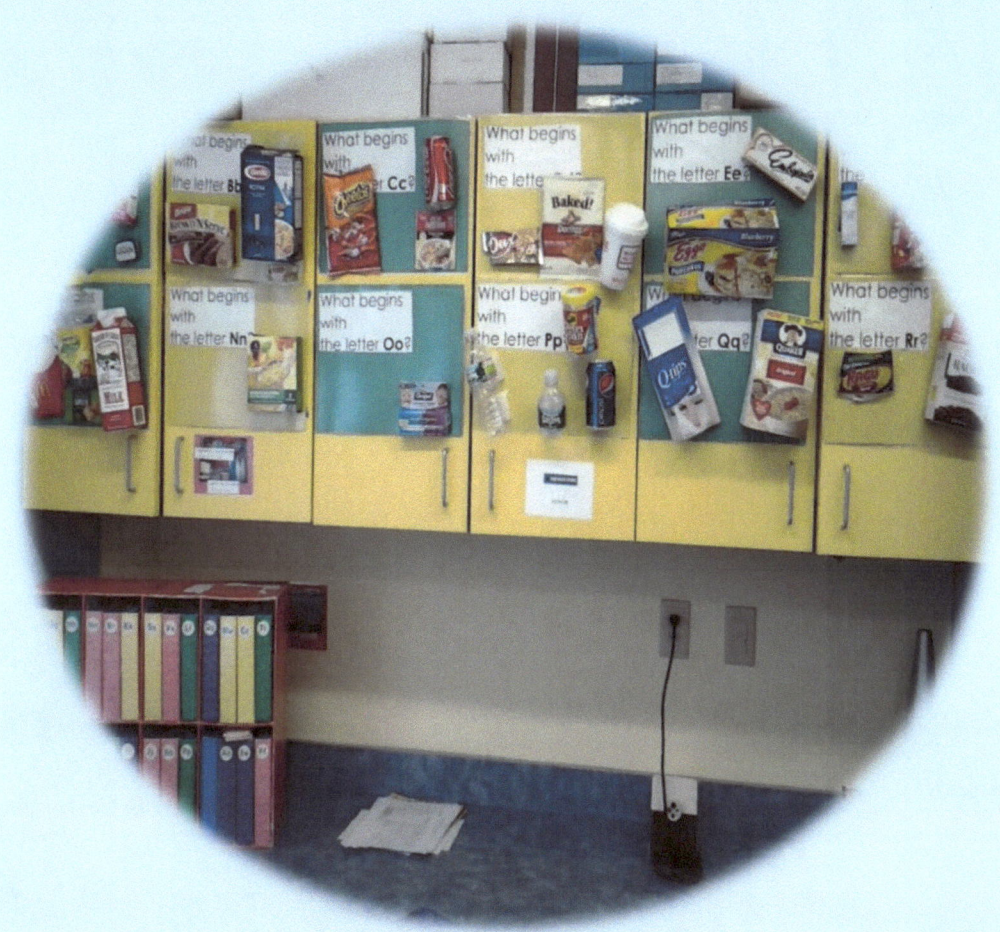

Here is an idea to use grocery items for an environmental print board.

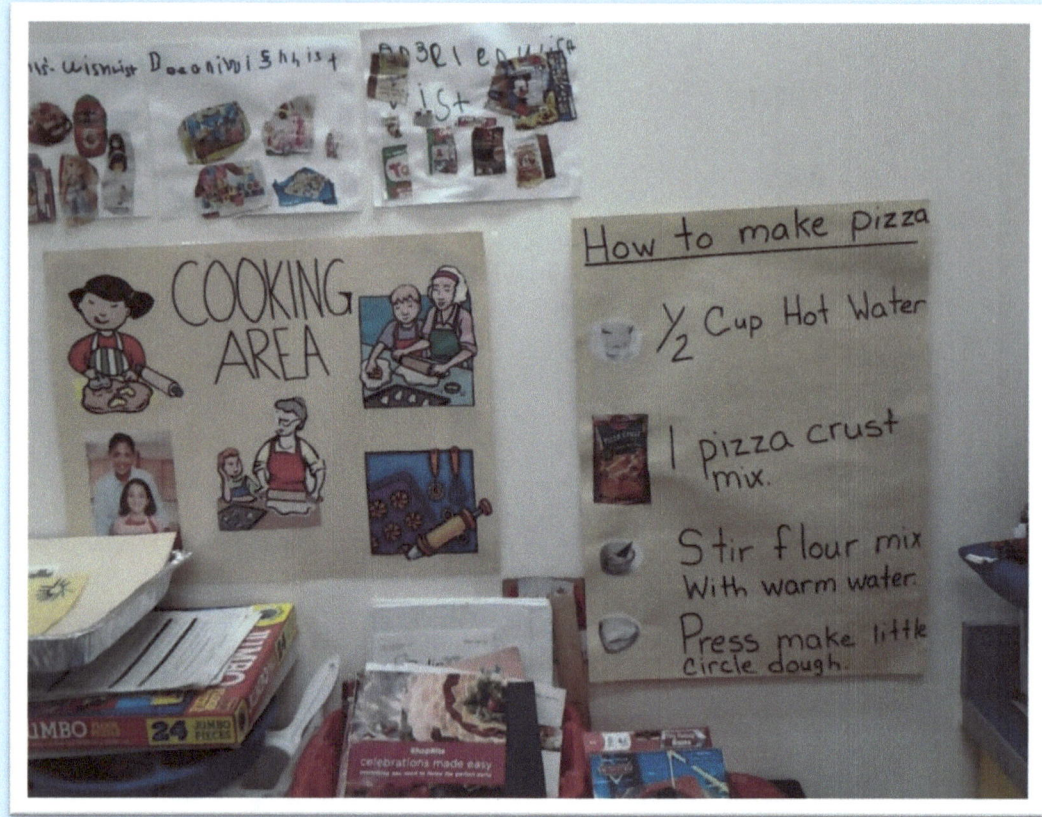

The cooking area displays pictures of various recipes along with the step by step directions.

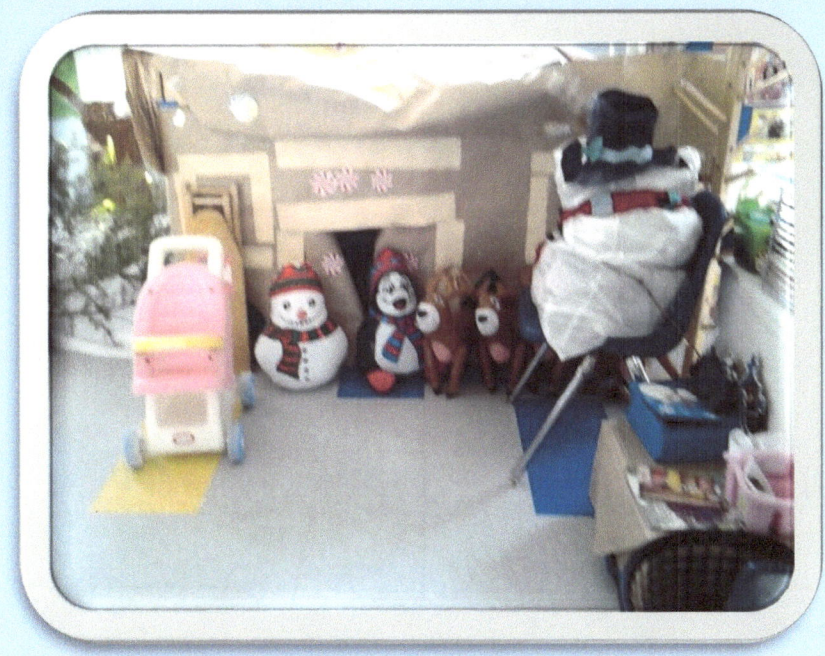

The dramatic play area changed to a winter wonderland. Maintain elements of the cooking area for integration of other studies.

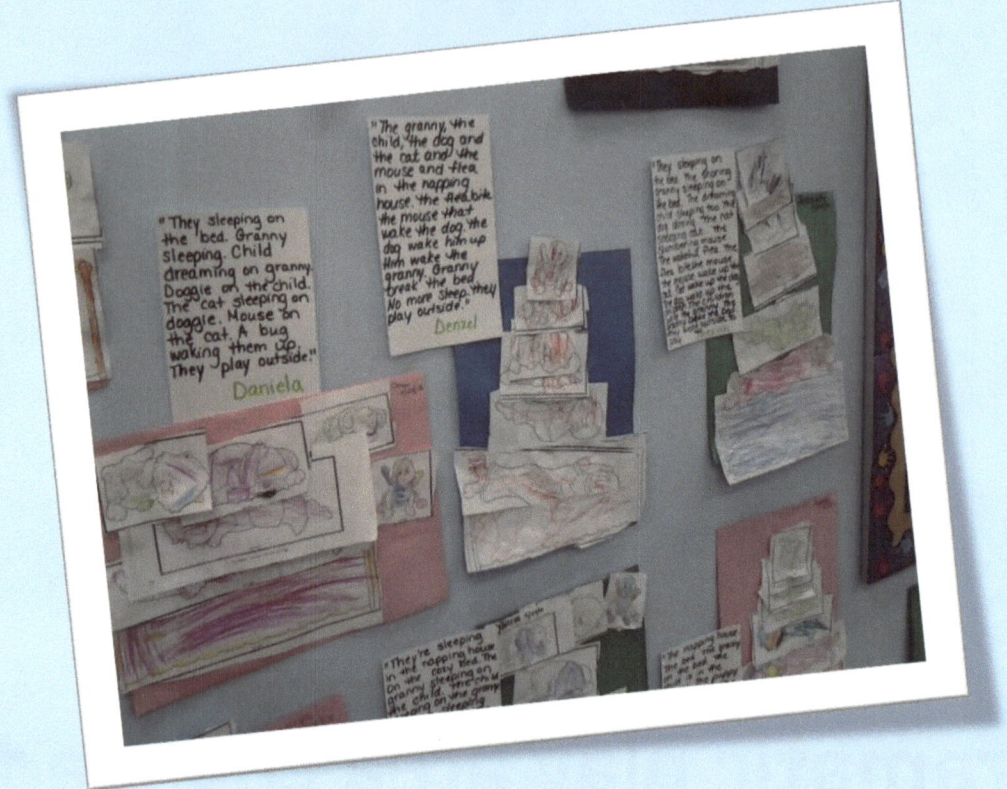

Dictations were taken by the preschool teacher of children's thoughts about their artwork.

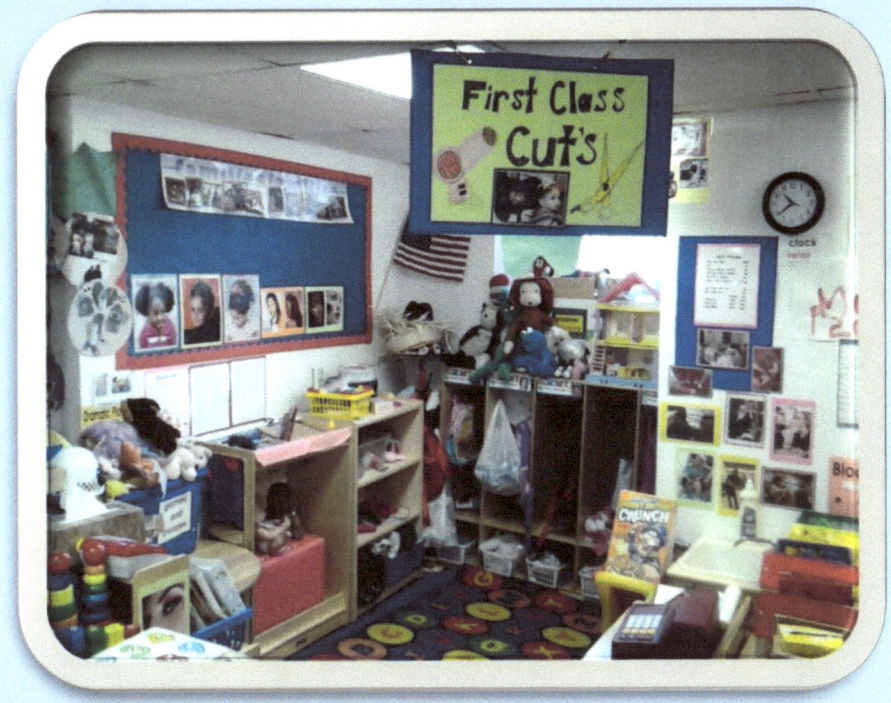

The dramatic play area changed to a hair salon. Notice the personal touches the preschool teacher has added.

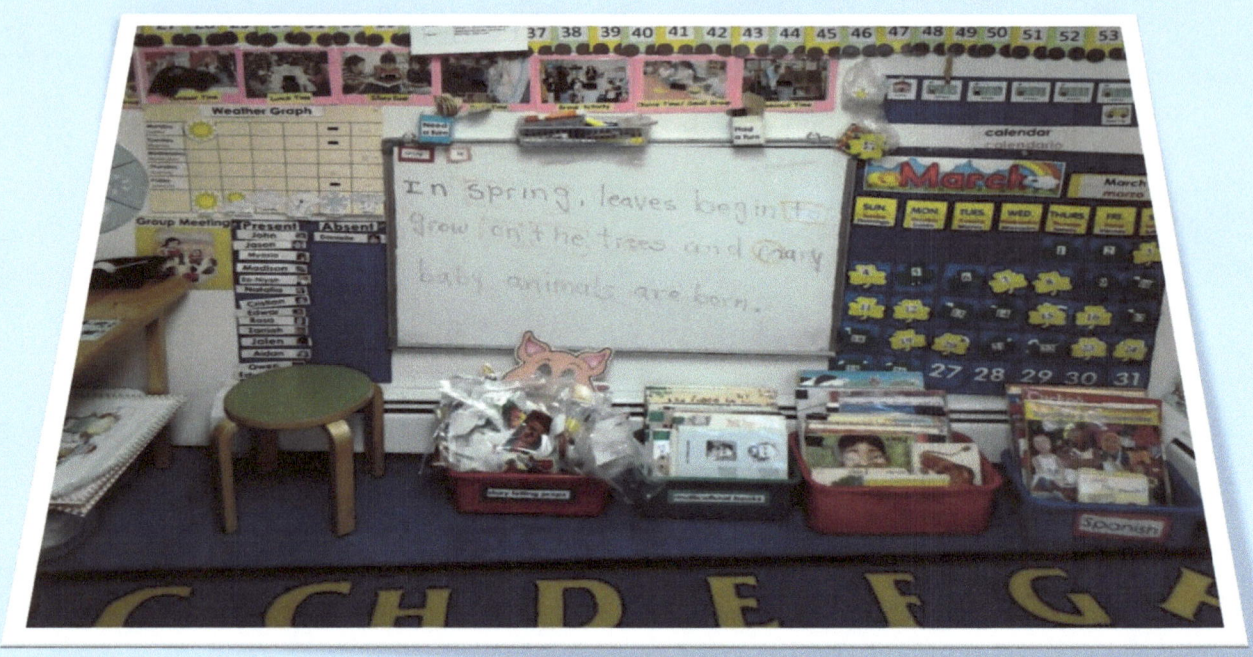

The writing area contains various writing tools and other posters at children's eye level.

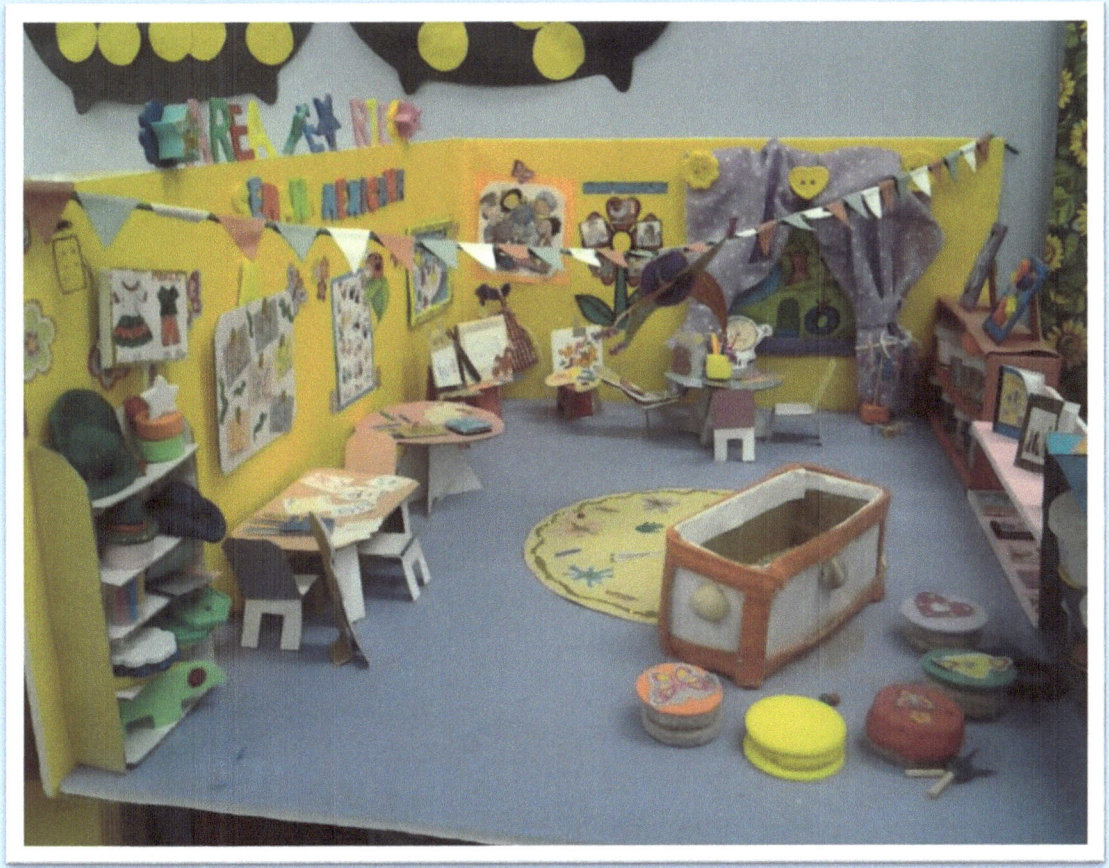

3D artwork

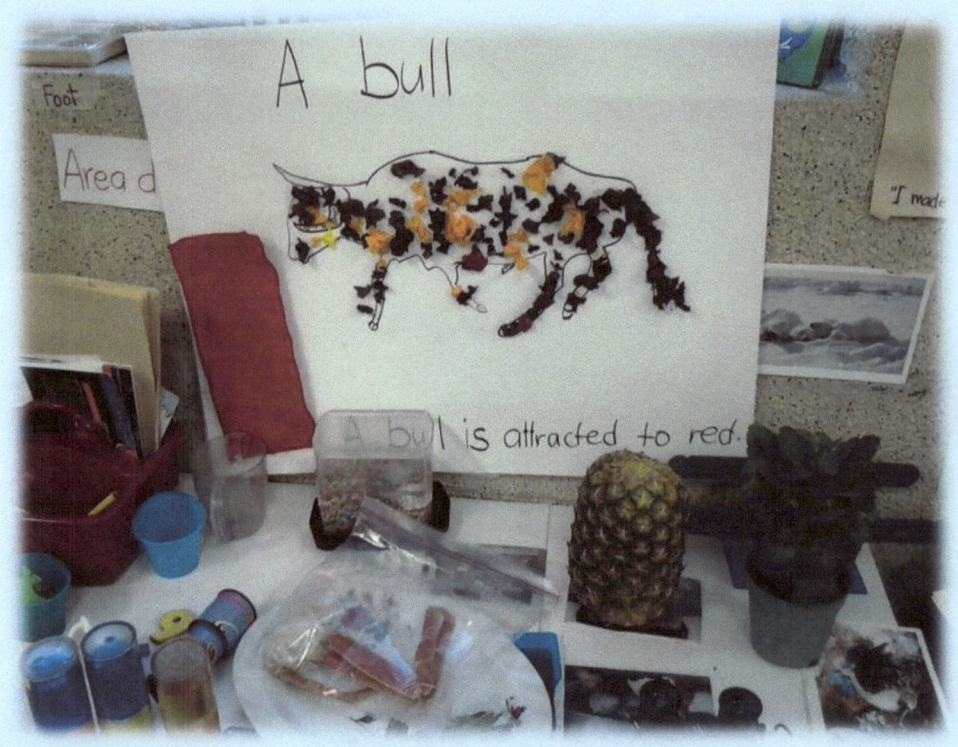

Discovery area displays detail facts children learned about a bull: "A bull is attracted to red." Write the child's name who pointed this out.

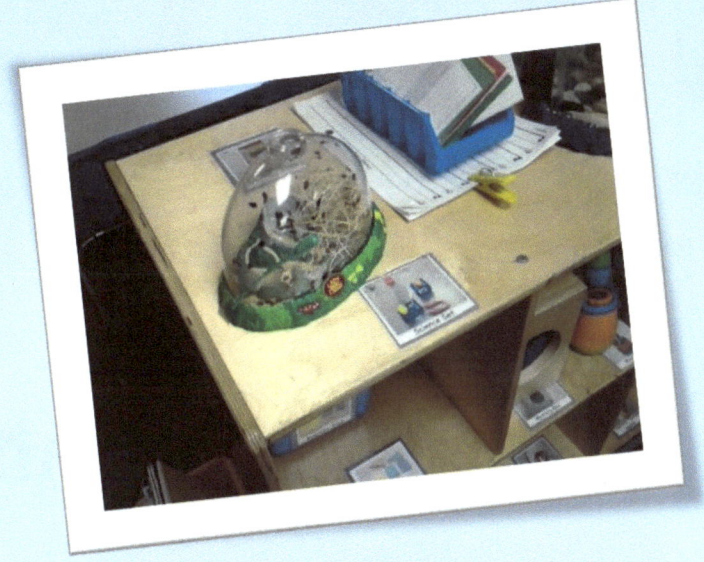

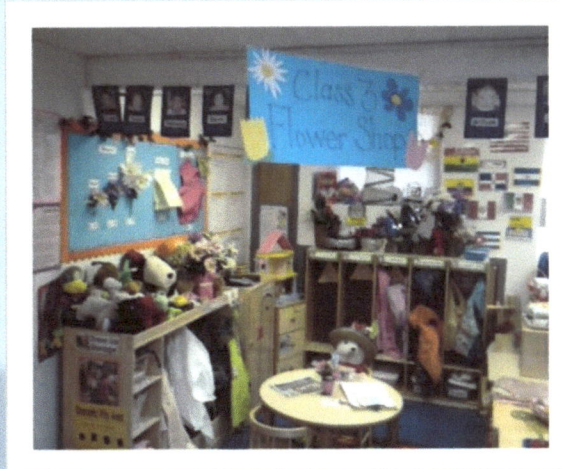

The dramatic play area is transformed into a flower shop.

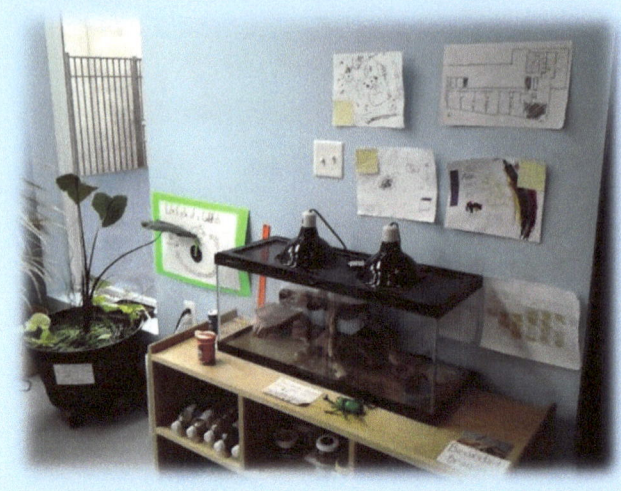

Greenhouse

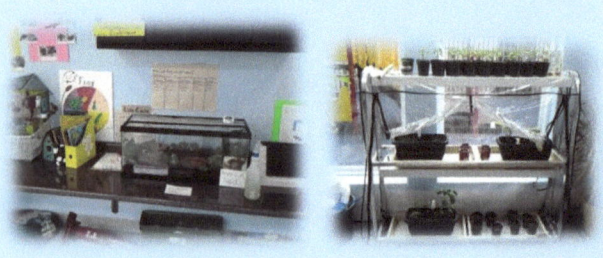

Plant display

Preschoolers' introduced to plants and how they reproduce.

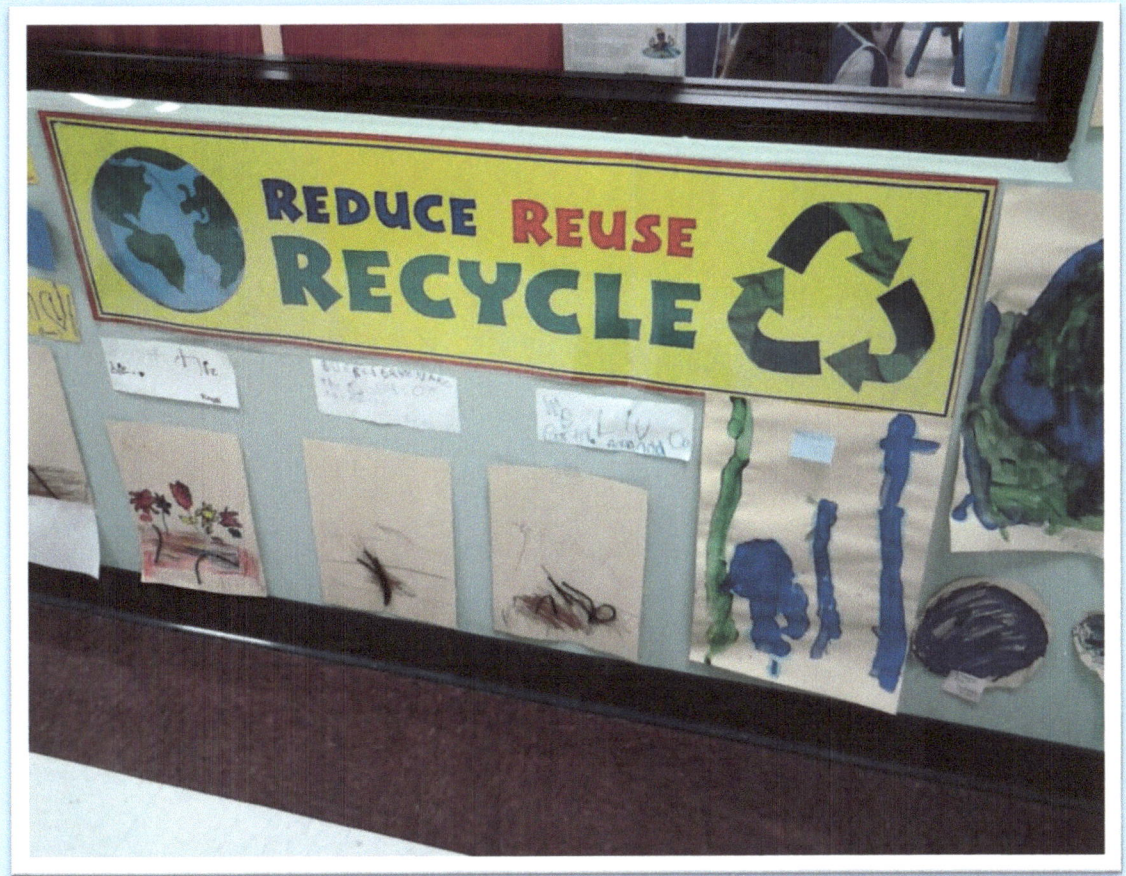

A display on how to reduce, reuse and recycle using pictures by preschoolers.

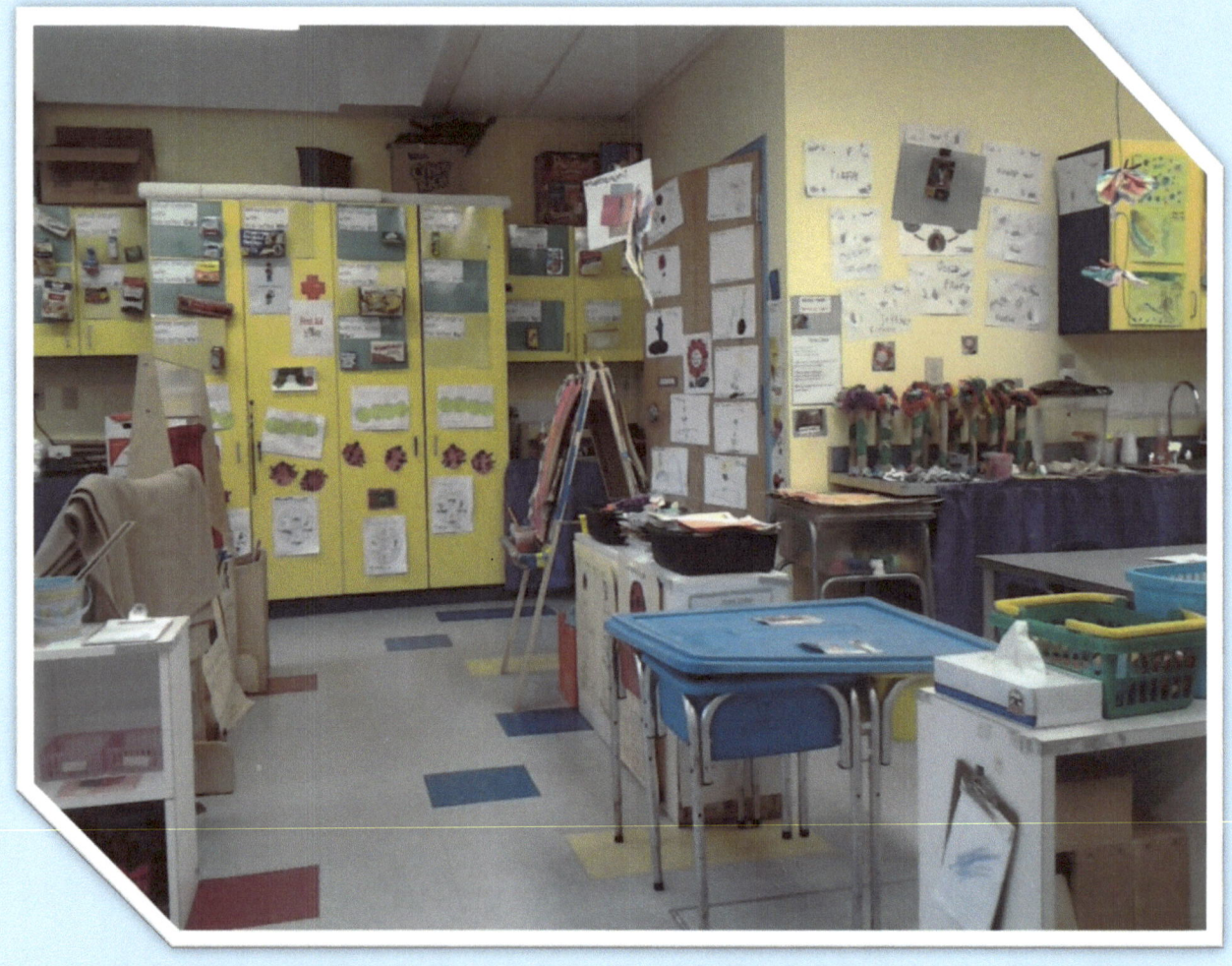

This is one way to use the space in a preschool environment for optimal use.

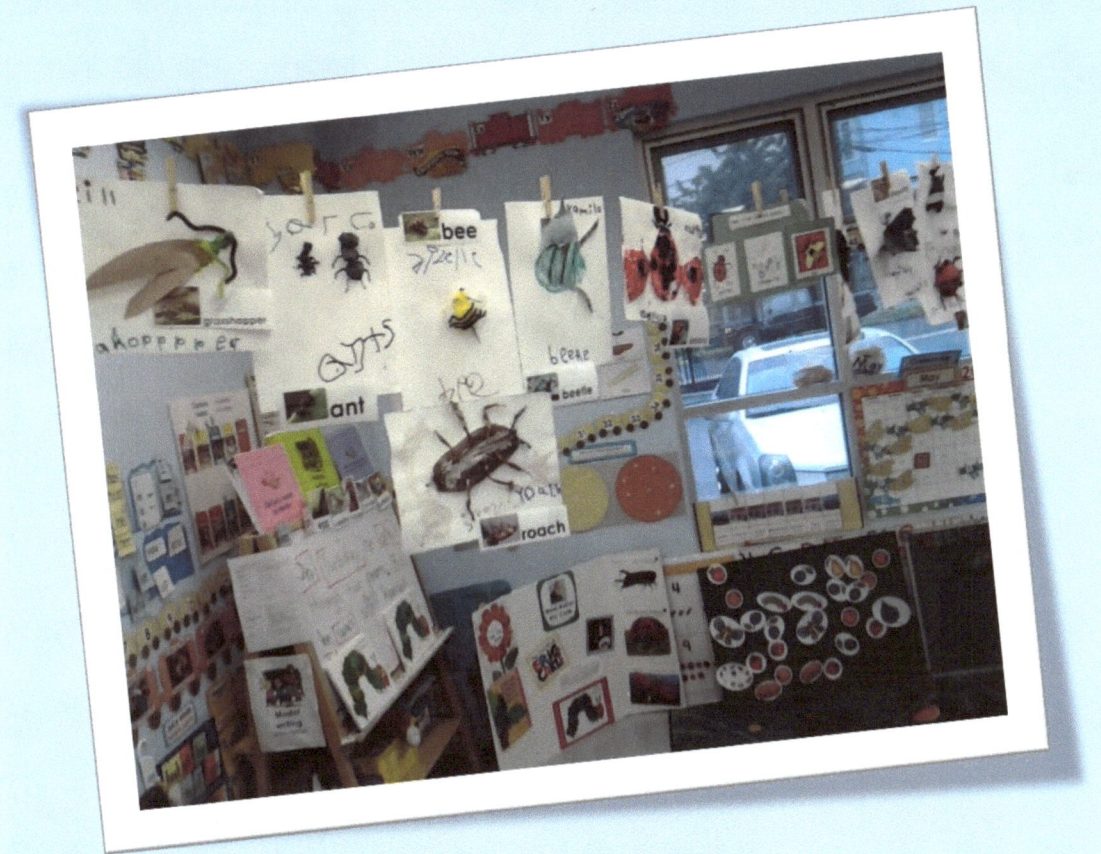

Insect investigation notice how the children's work is displayed and the use of the flannel board.

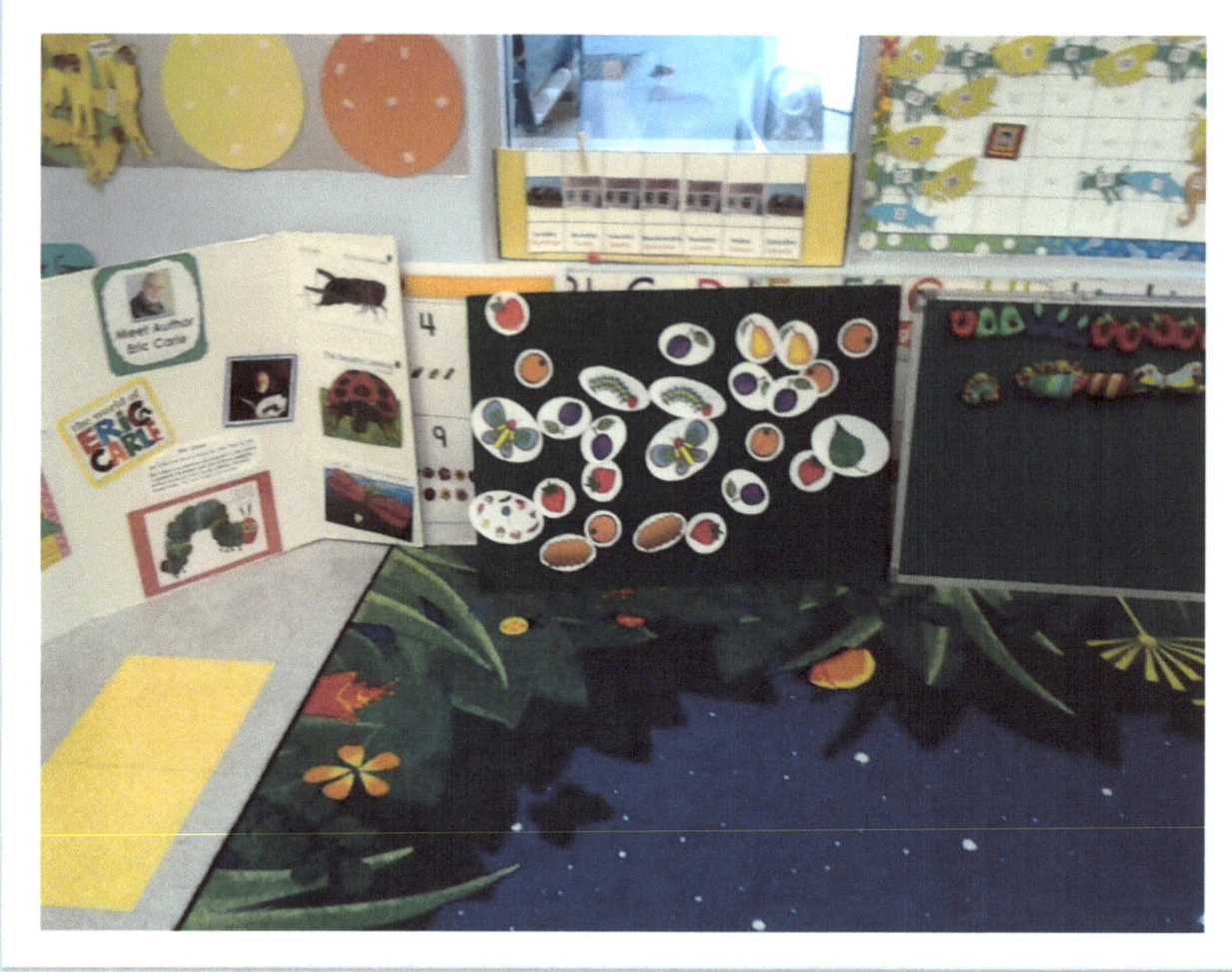

Flannel board ideas used with felt and cardboard pictures.

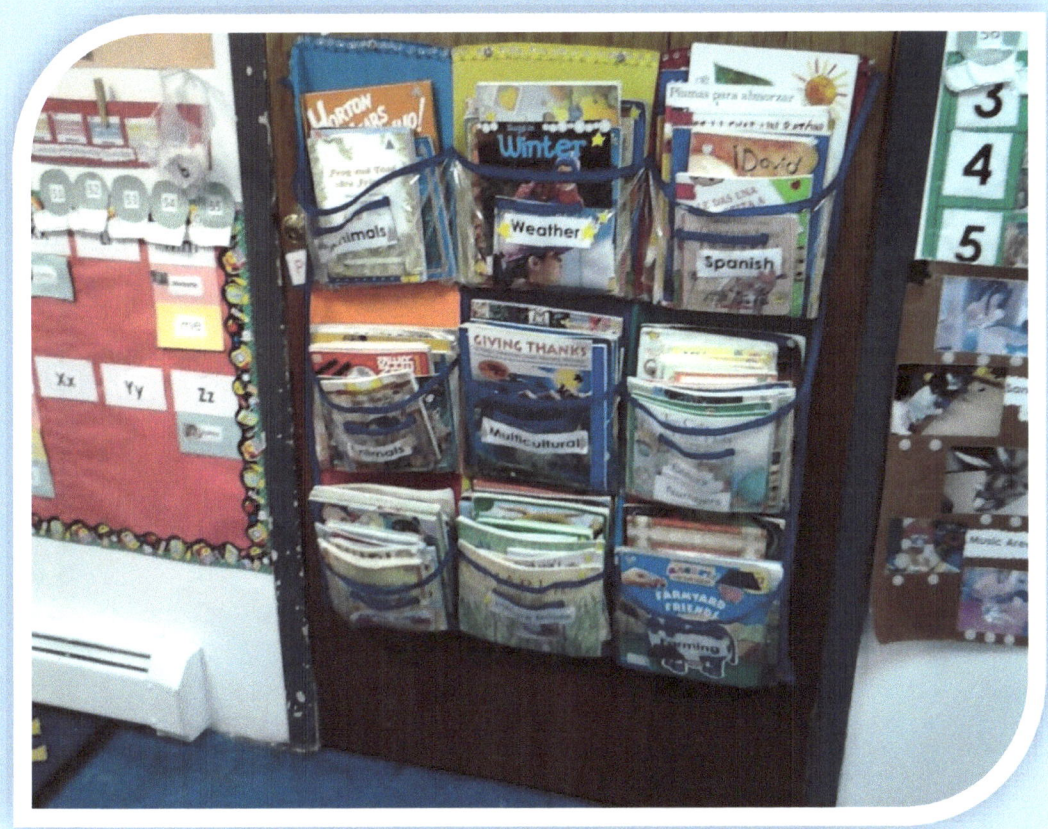

Library organization

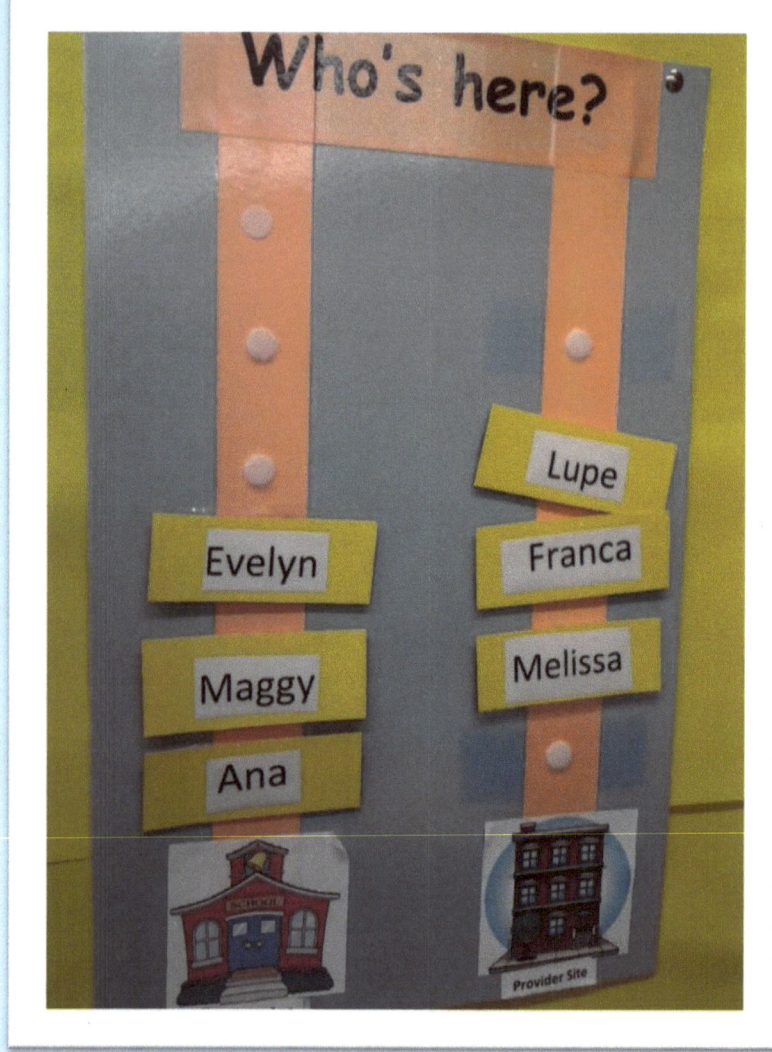

Attendance board

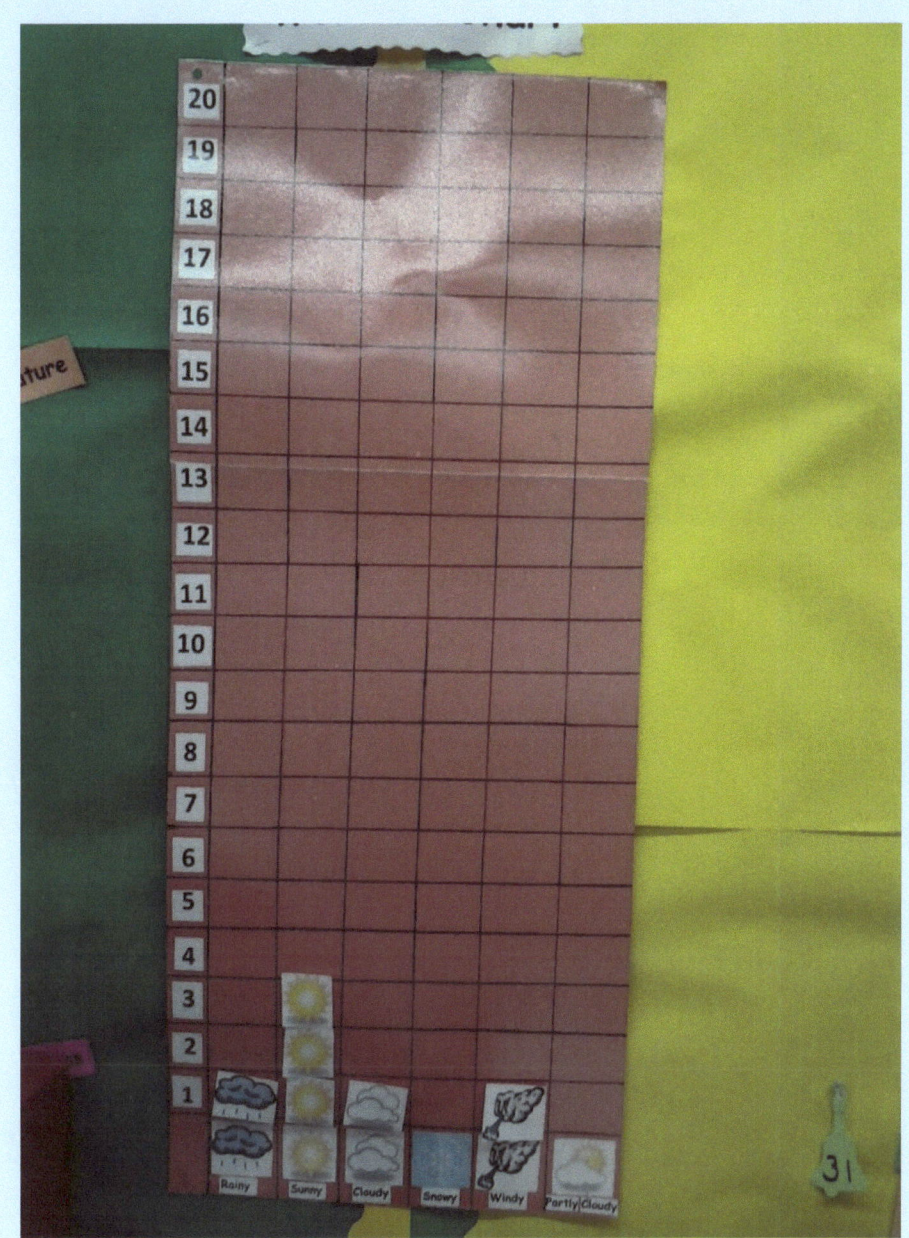

Weather graph

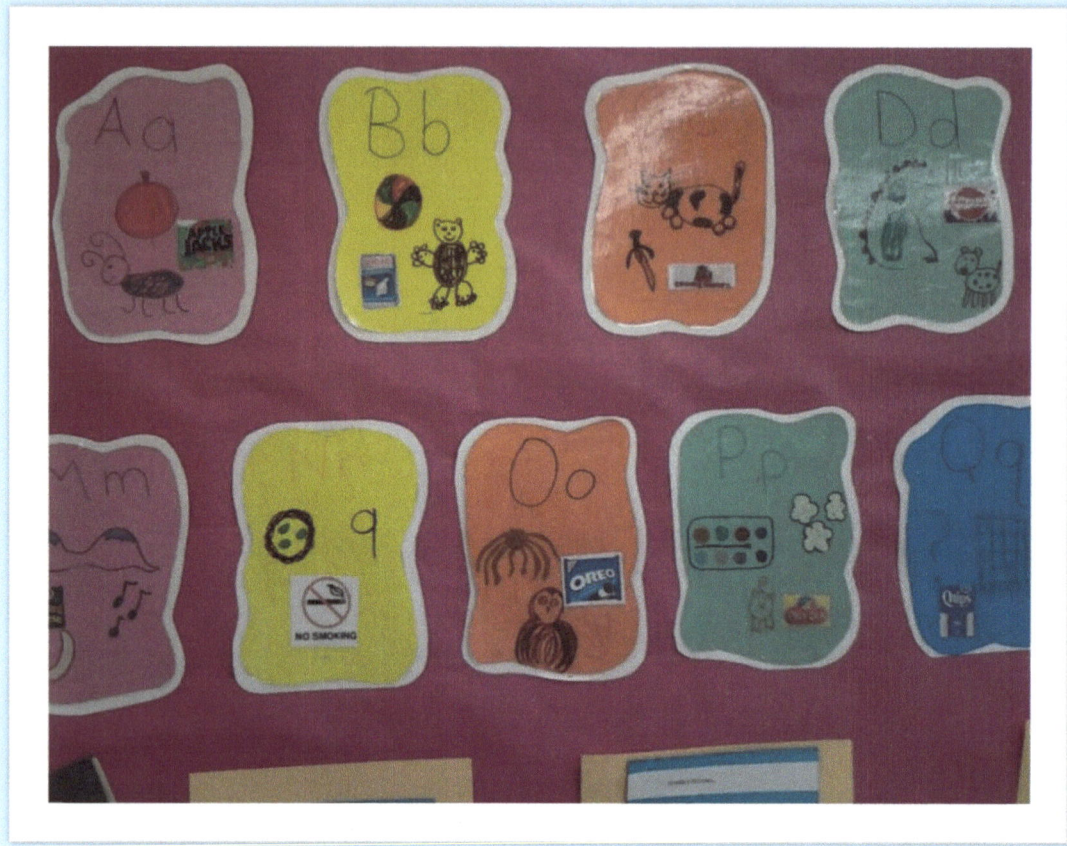

An environmental alphabet chart created using children's own drawings.

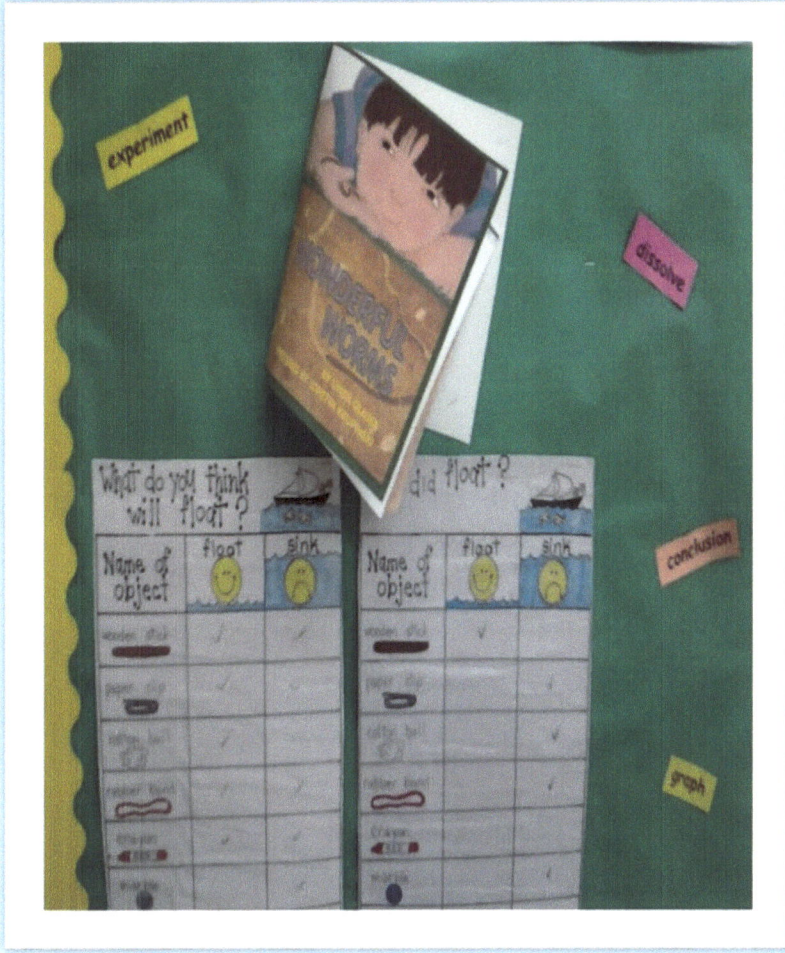

Float and sink investigations in the discovery area.

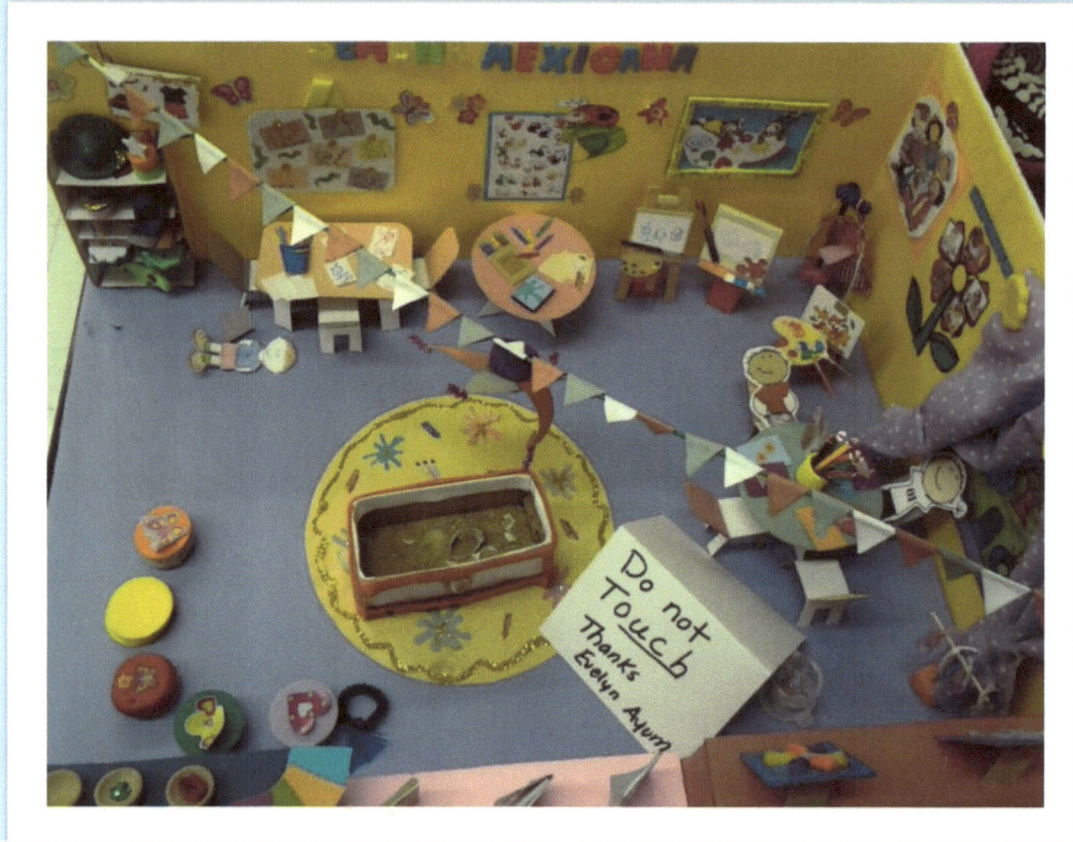

This is a parent's perspective of a preschool environment.

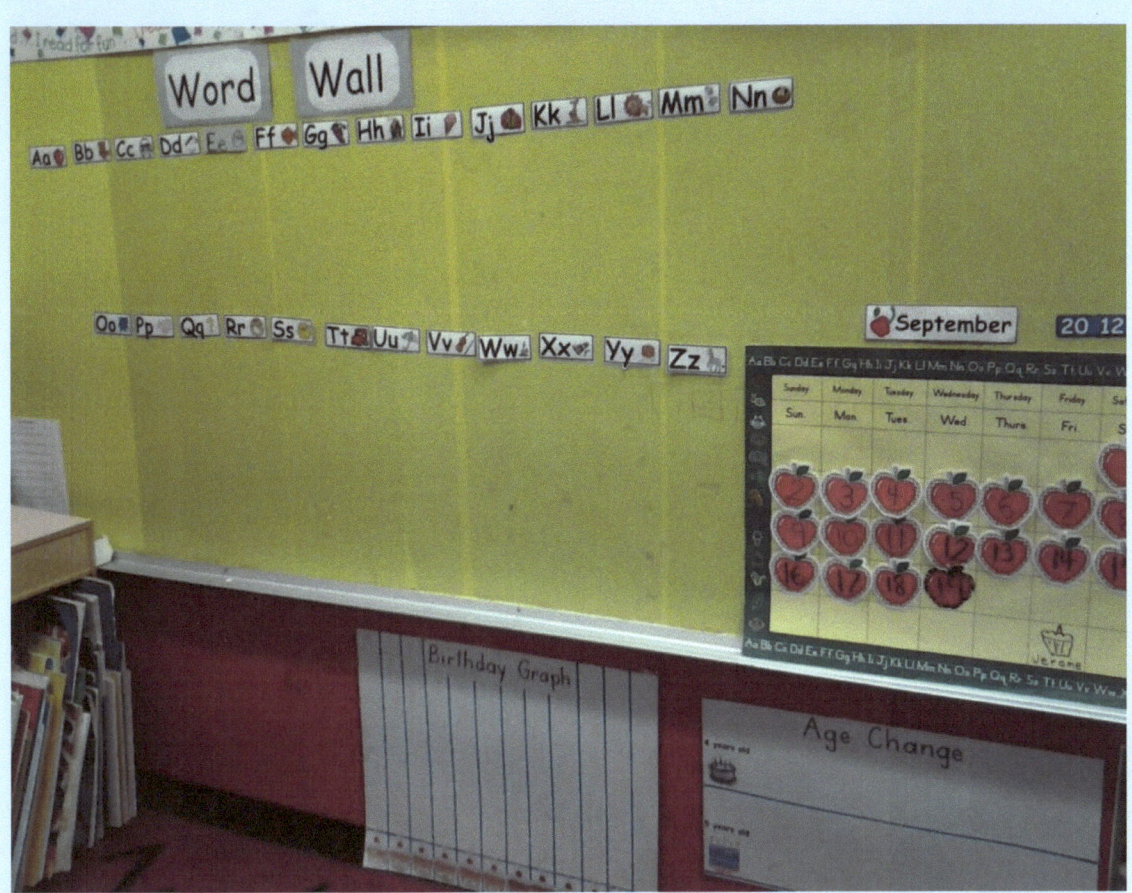

A word wall, calendar, birthday graph and age chart in a preschool environment.

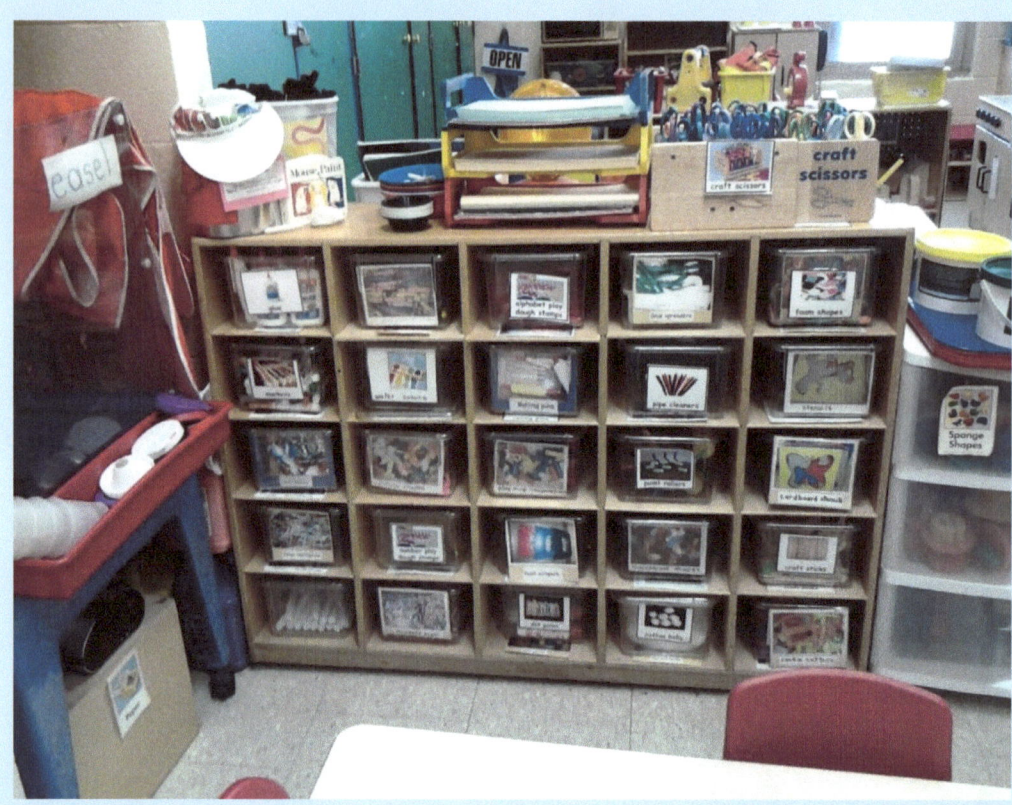

Here is an idea on how to label the bins, in the toys and games area with pictures and words for young learners to read.

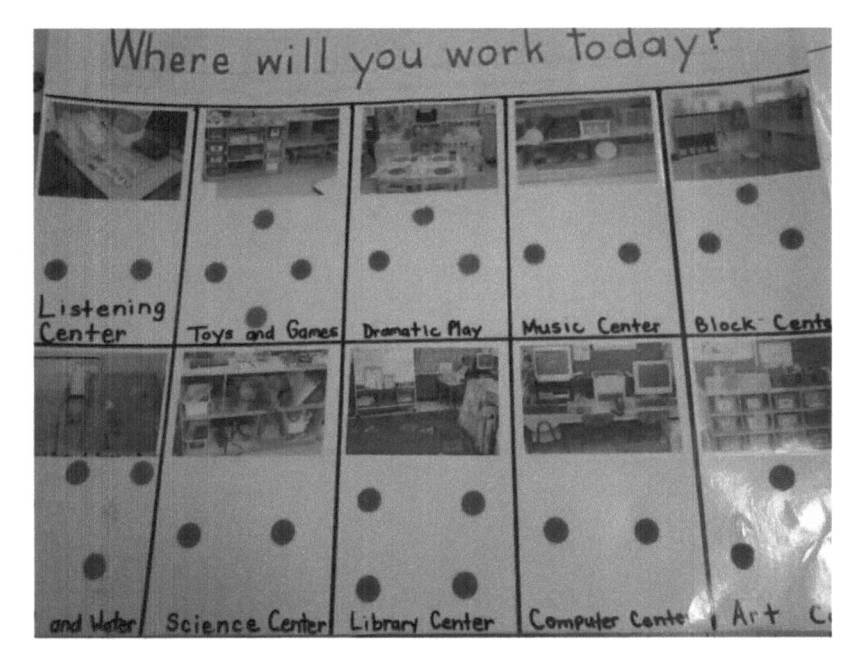

A planning board display using Velcro dots so children can place their pictures on and off when moving from one interest area to the next.

And for children to know how many can play in each interest area.

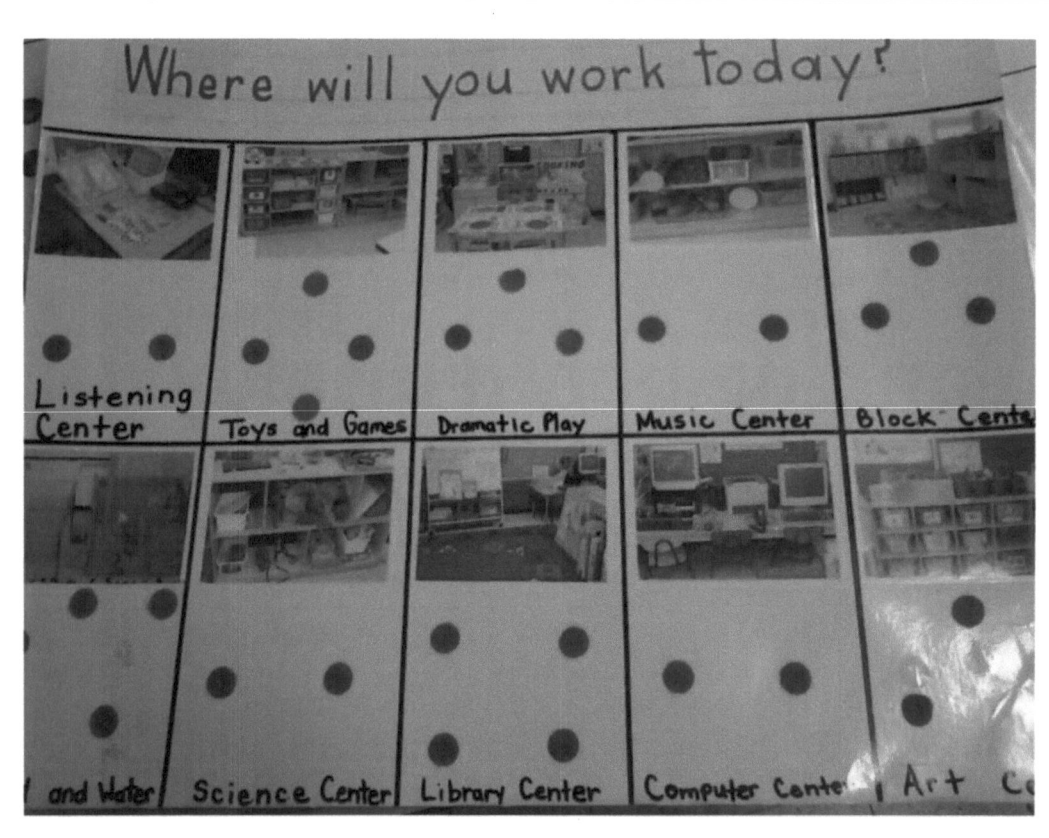

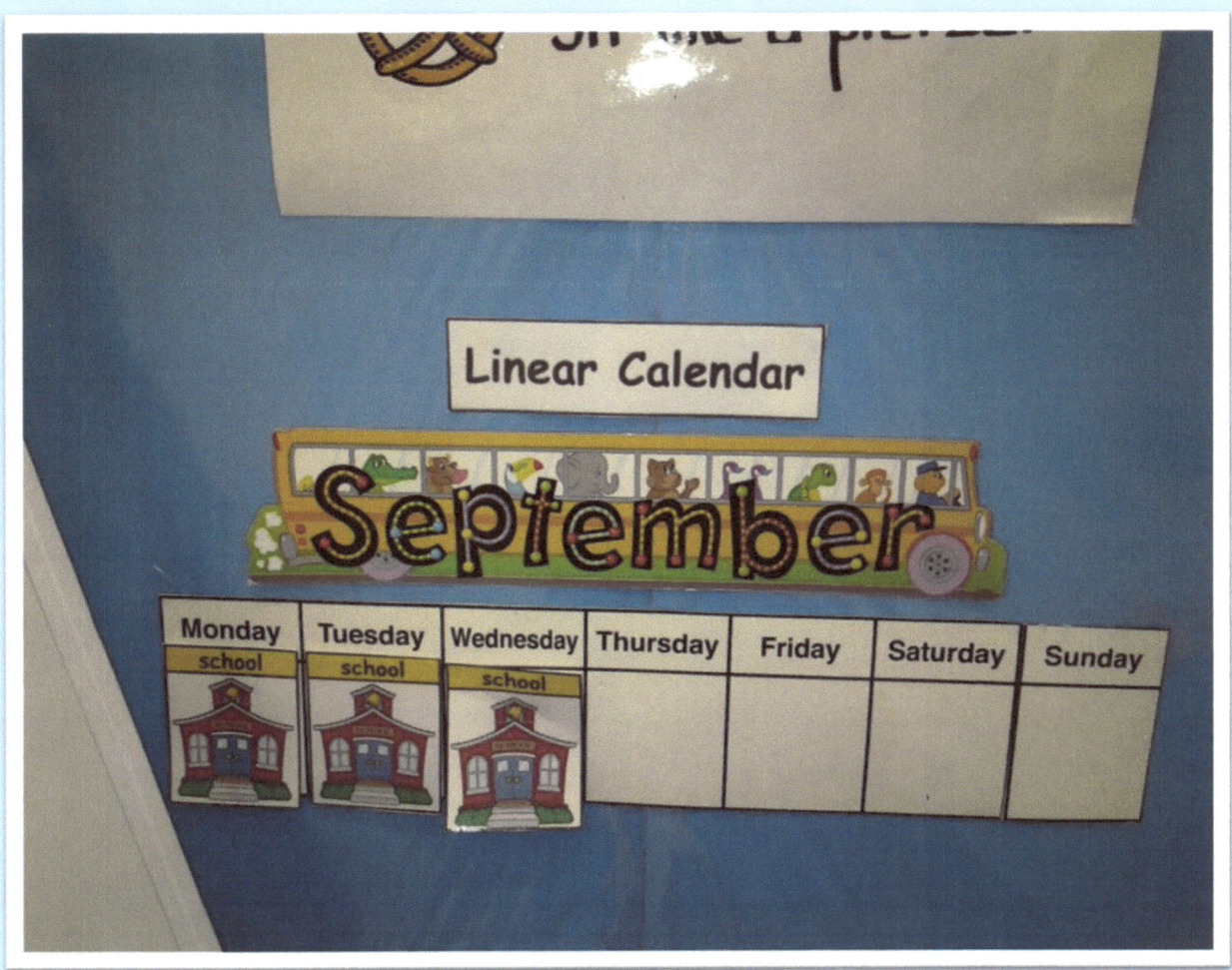

Linear calendar for younger preschoolers.

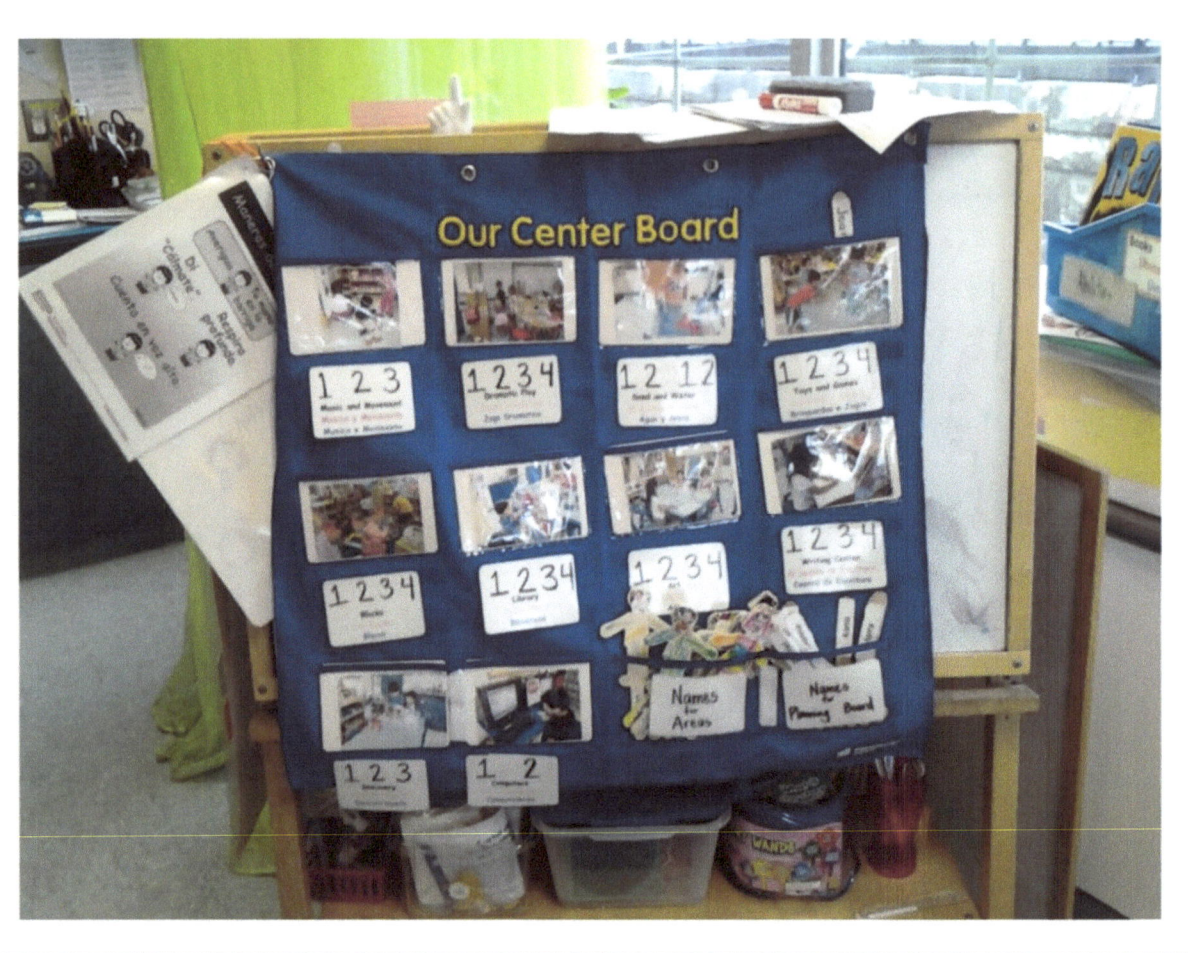

Planning board labeled "Our Center Board."

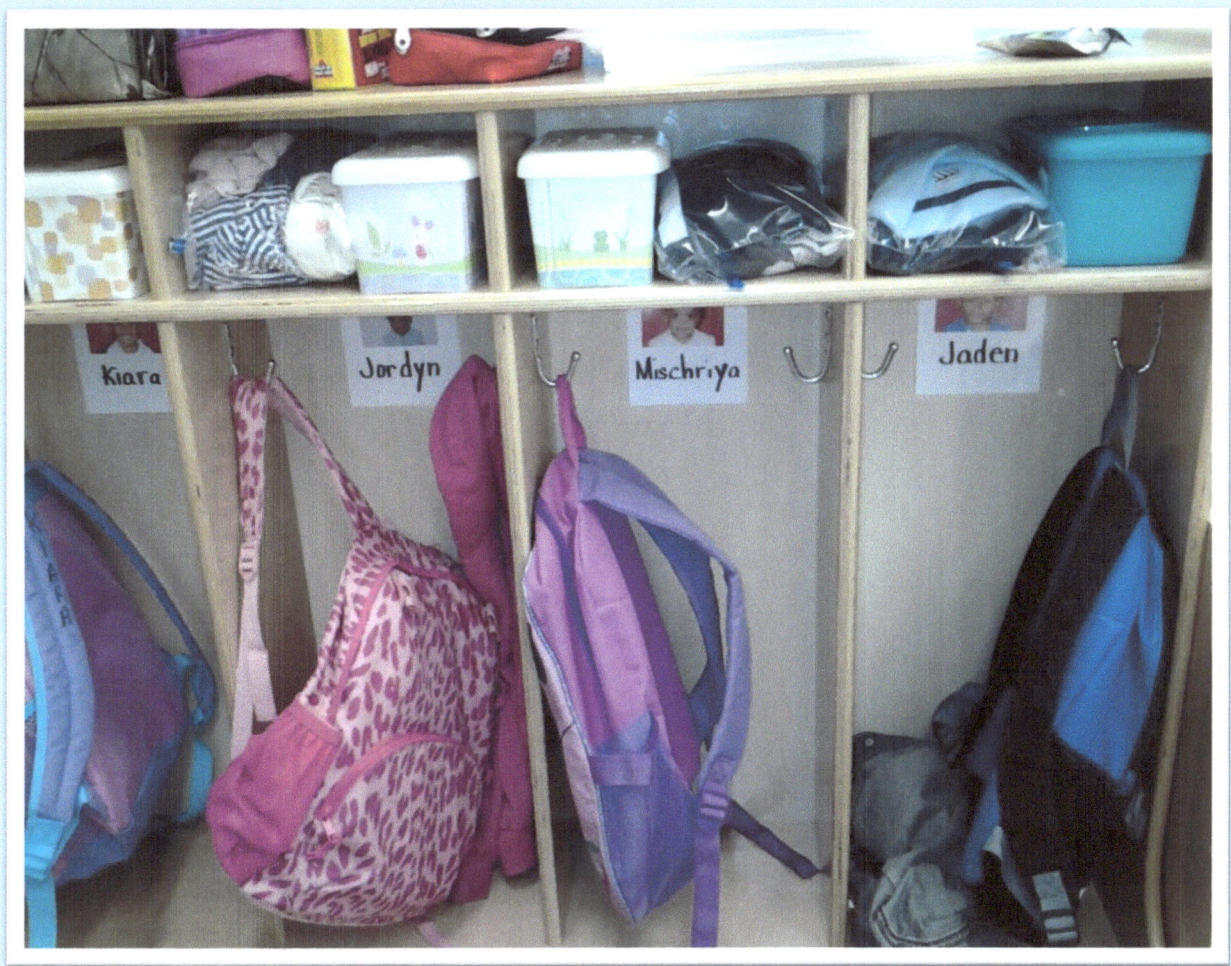

Cubbies labeled with words and pictures.

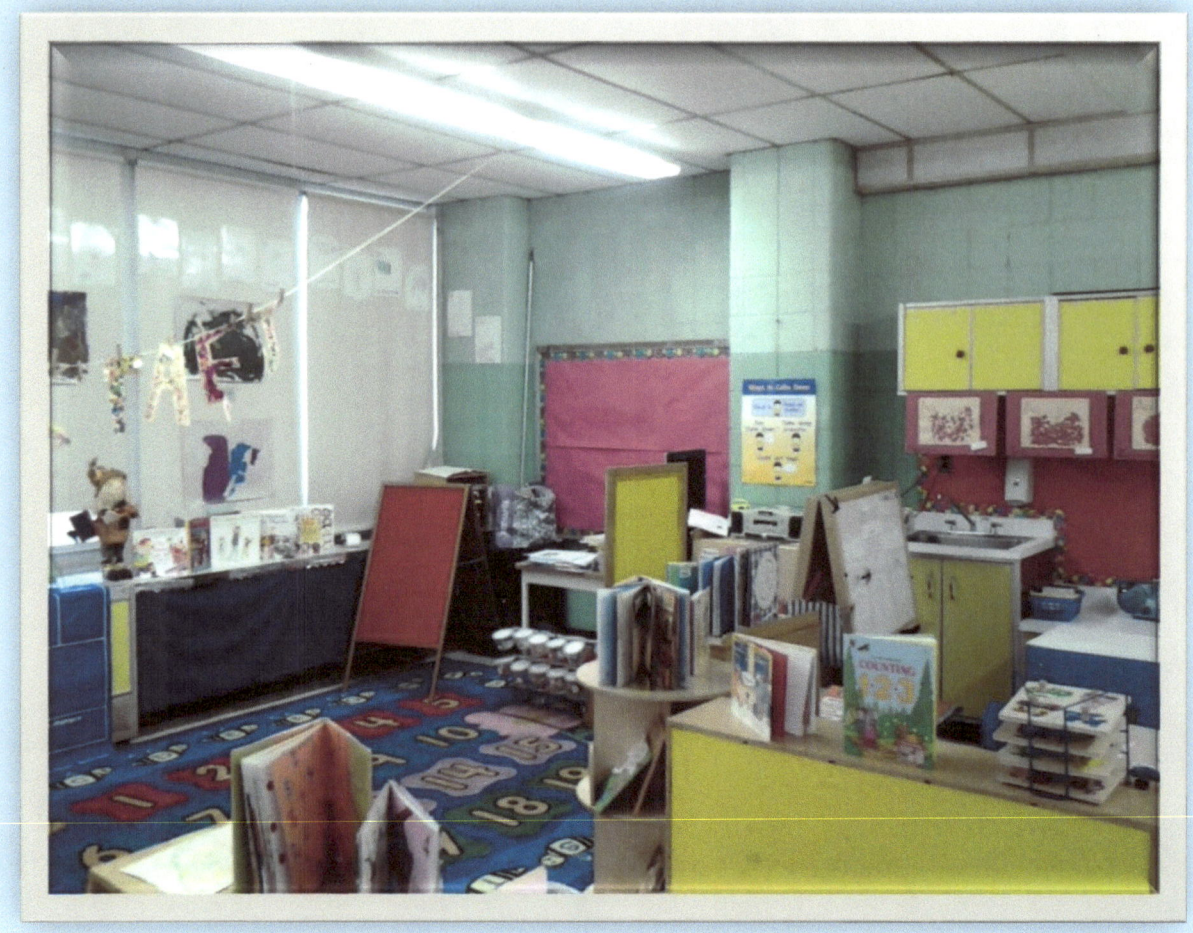

A preschool environment filled with literacy items.

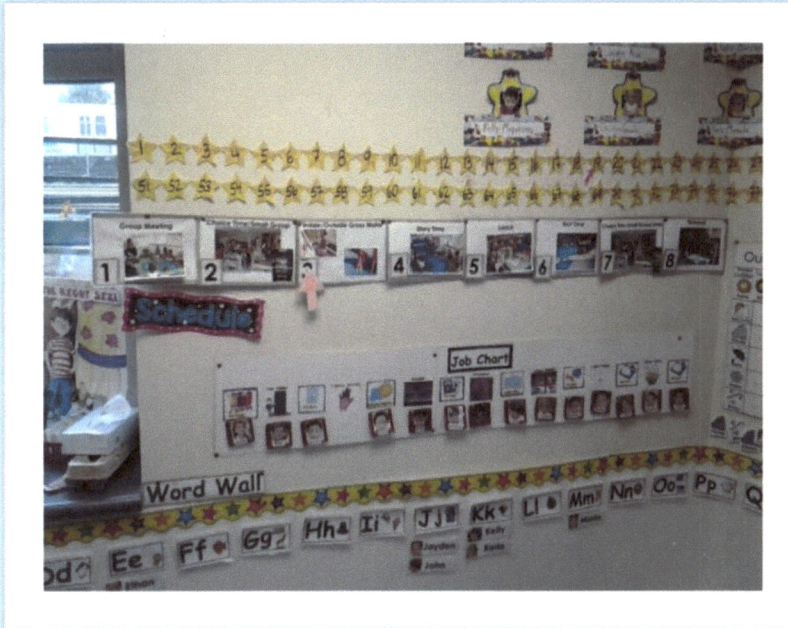

A display of the children's schedule, job chart and word

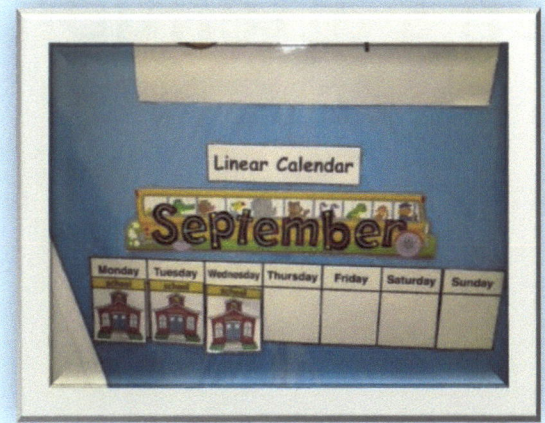

wall.

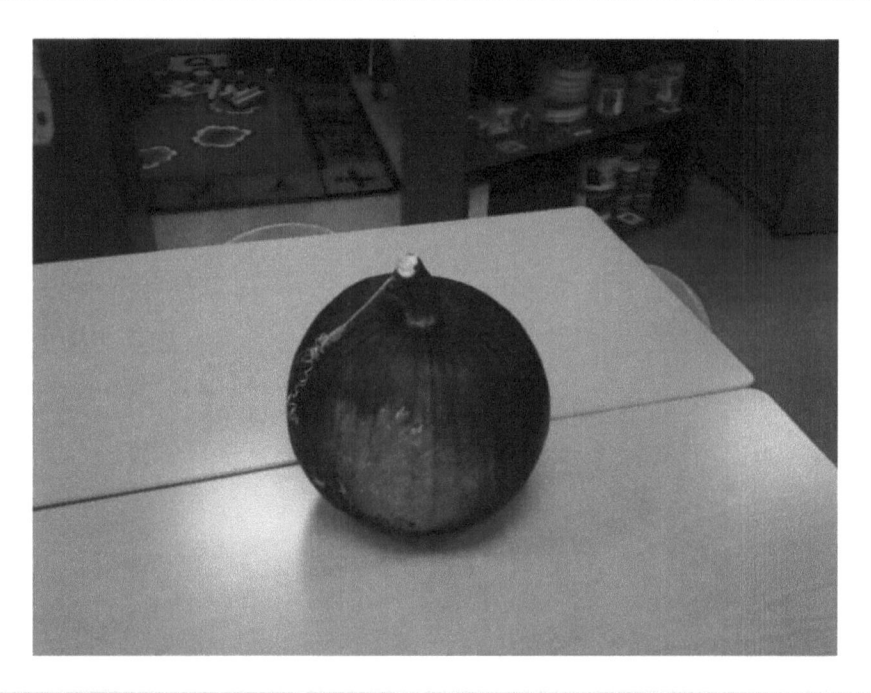

Display the unusual to get children's attention.

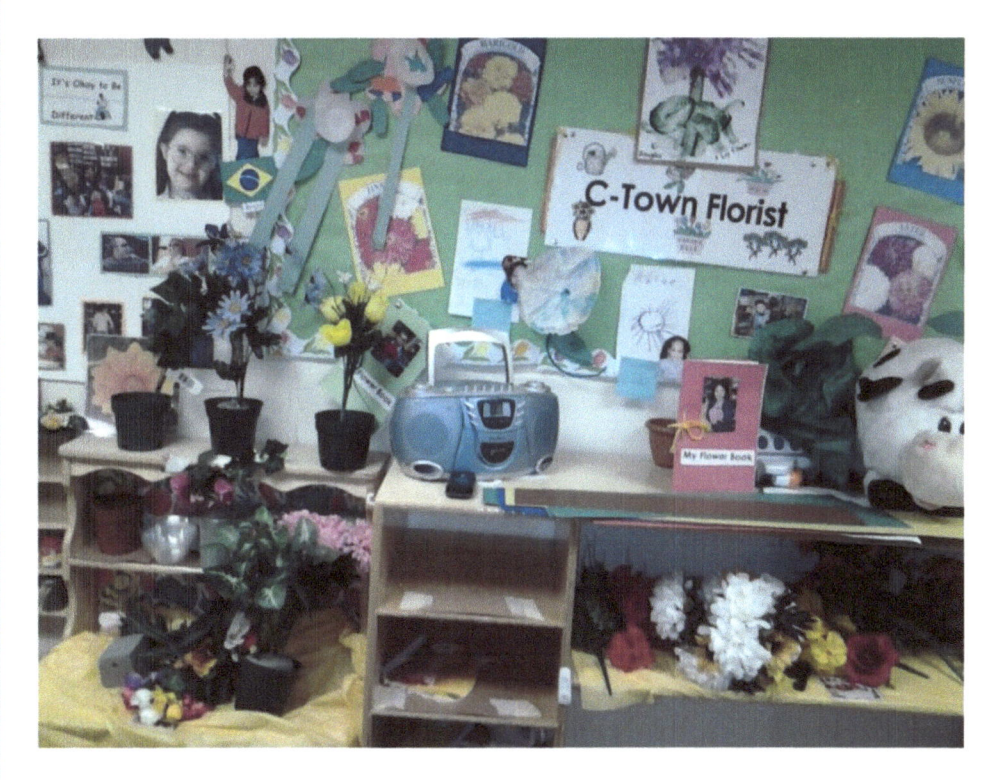

Dramatic play changes to a flower shop.

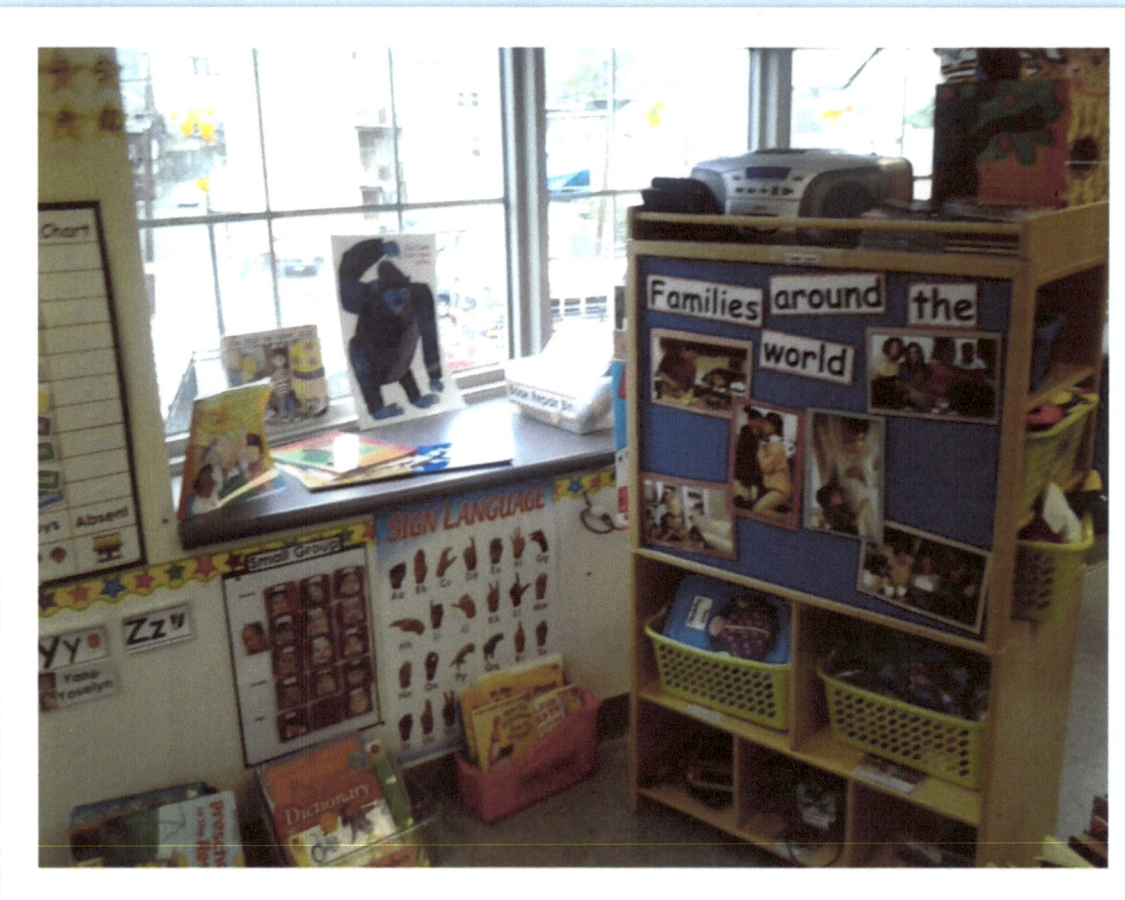

Here is a multicultural display of families from around the world in the library area.

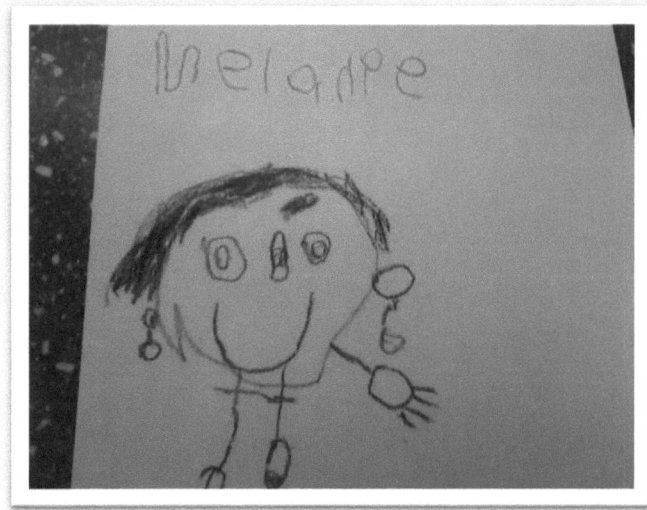

A child's artwork

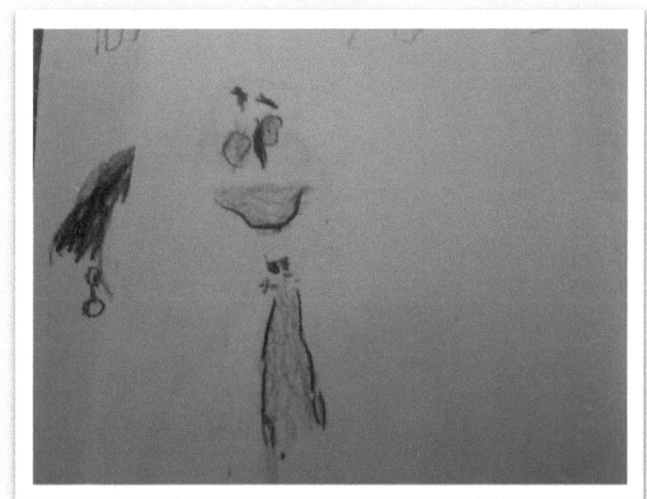

The artwork is called "This is my face" created by a four-year-old.

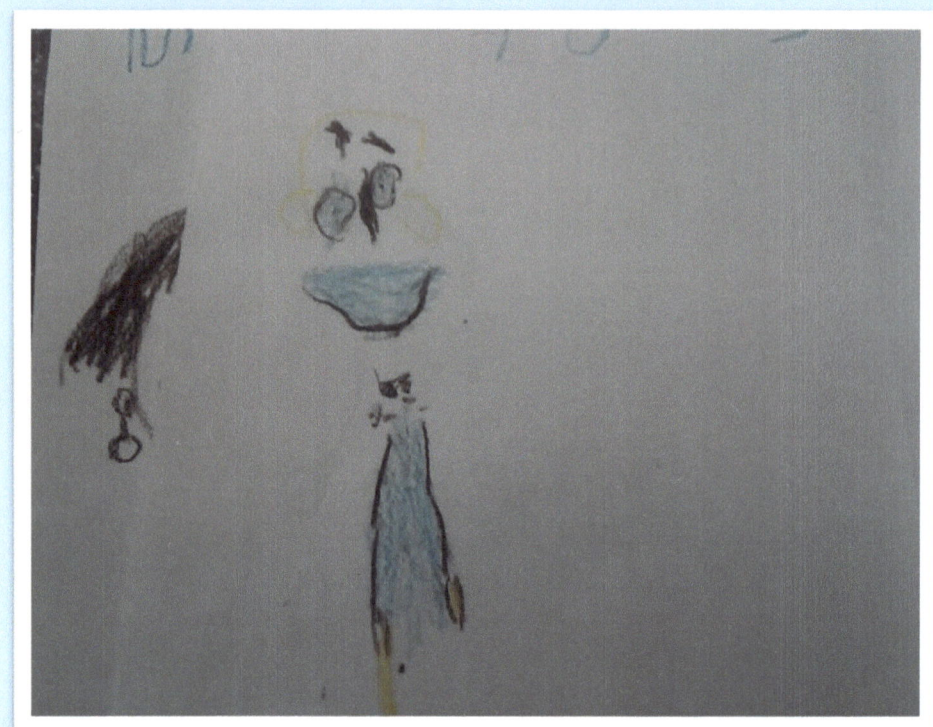

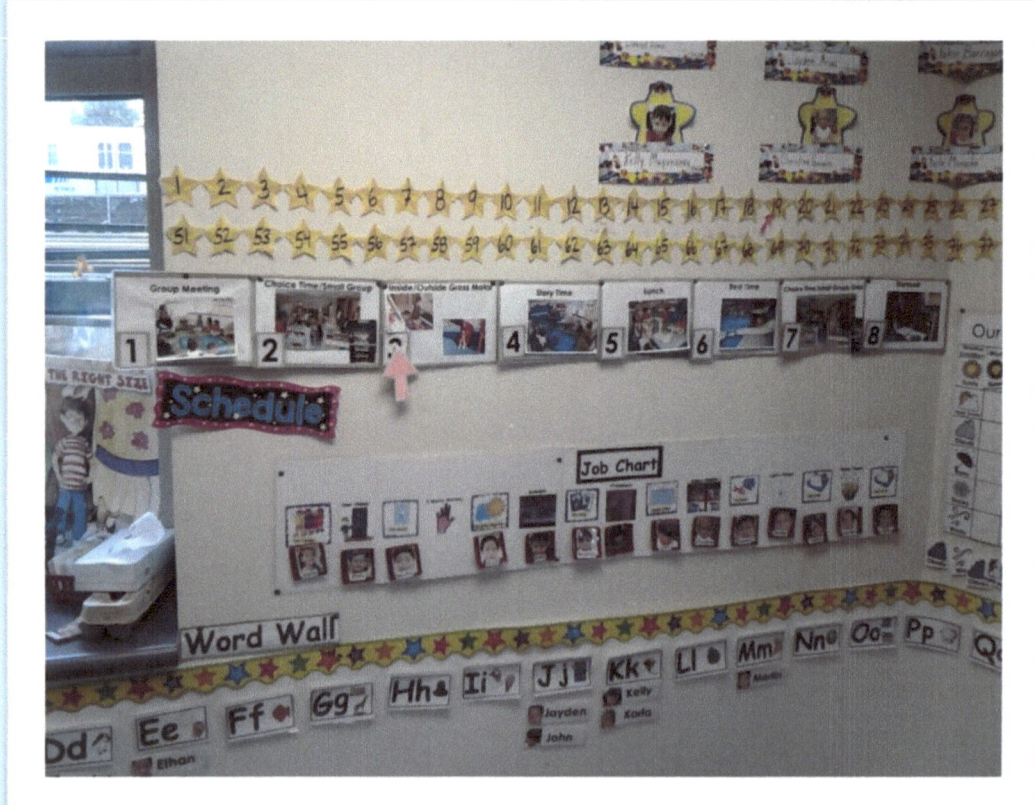

Displayed are posters of a children's schedule with pictures, a job chart, a weather chart and a word wall.

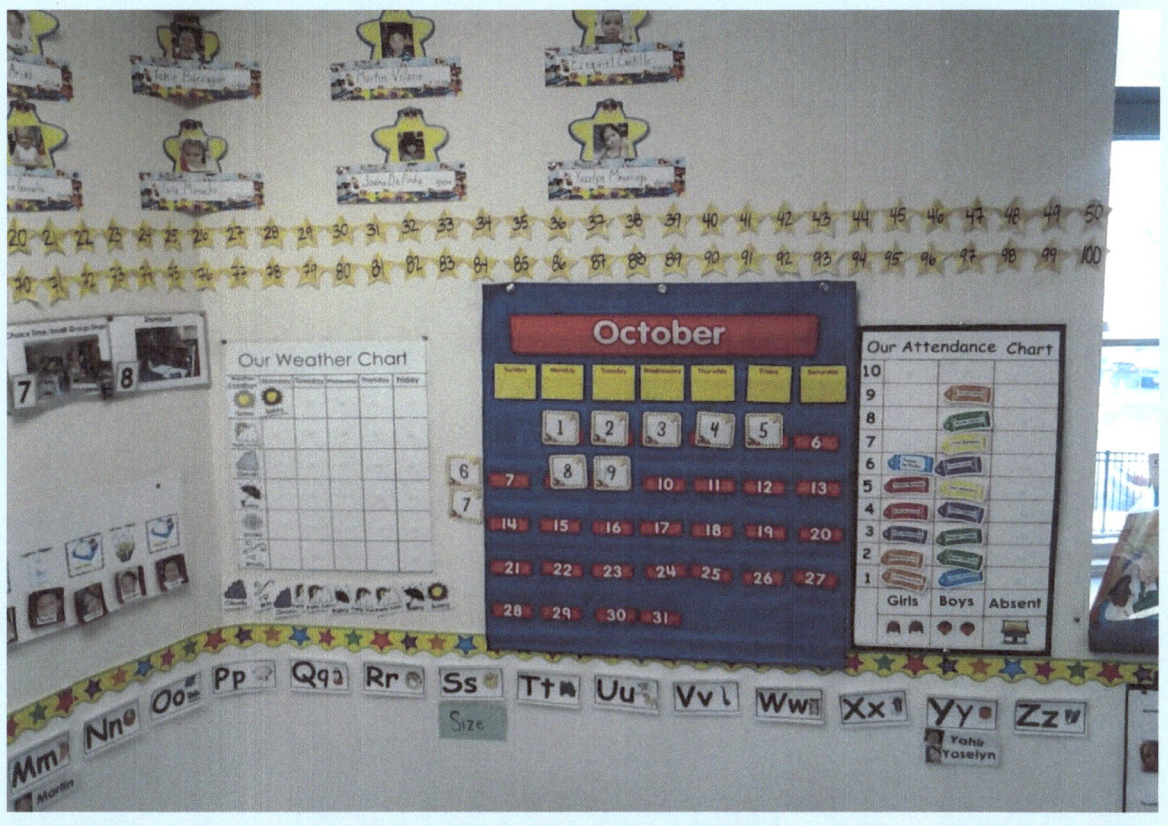

Posters of daily routines notice how the space is used wisely,

so that the teacher can access at children's eye level.

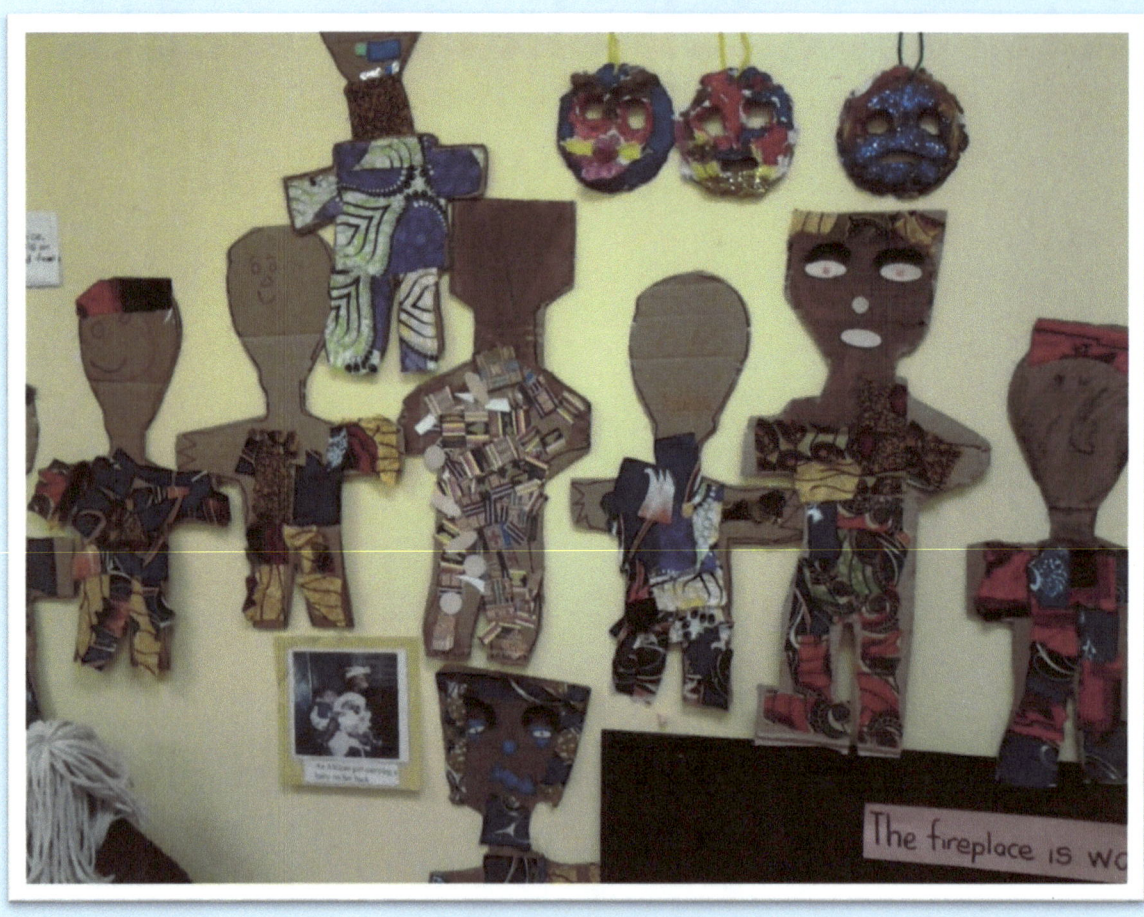

These are multicultural images created with cardboard paper notice the individual designs.

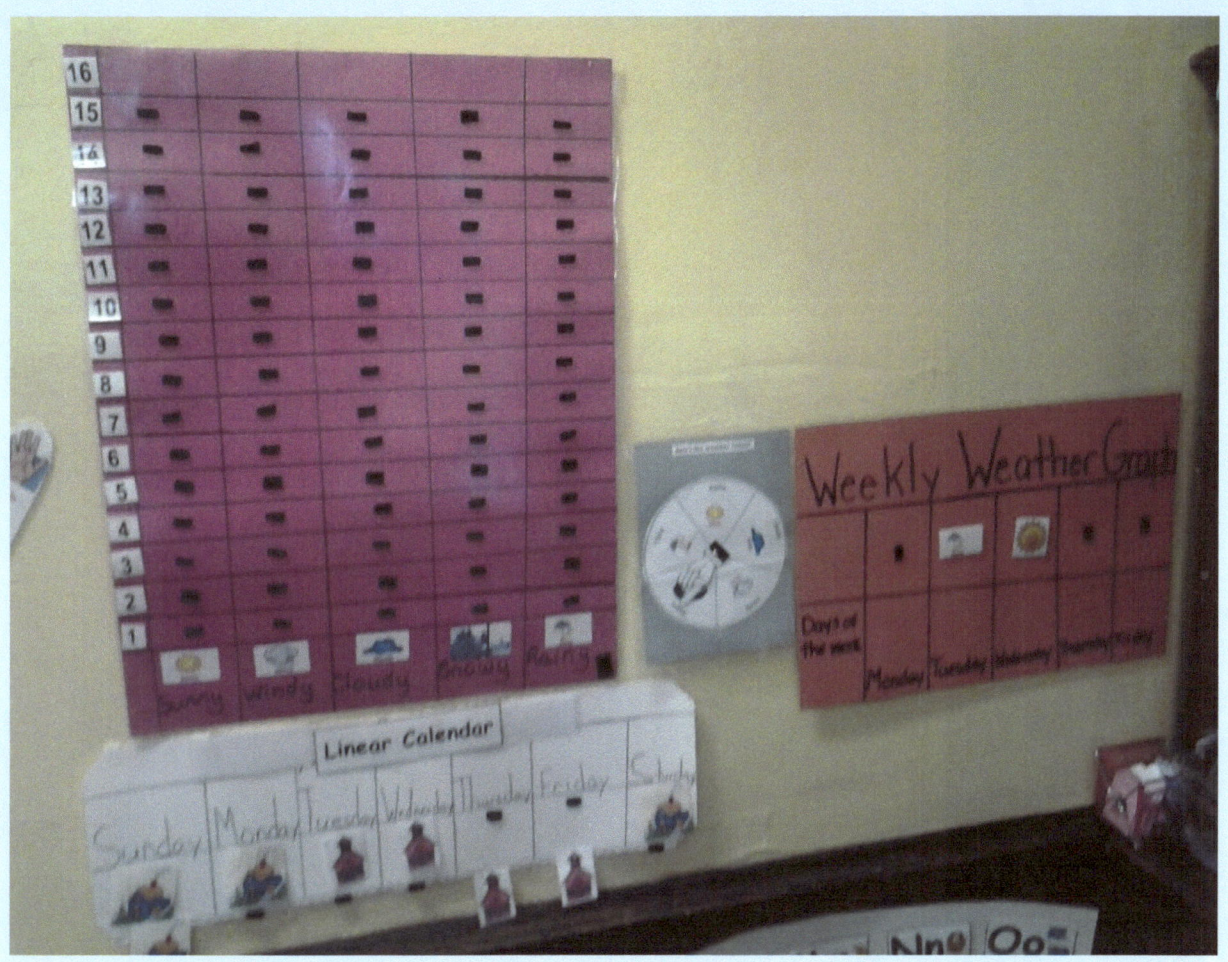

Weekly weather chart graph and linear calendar.

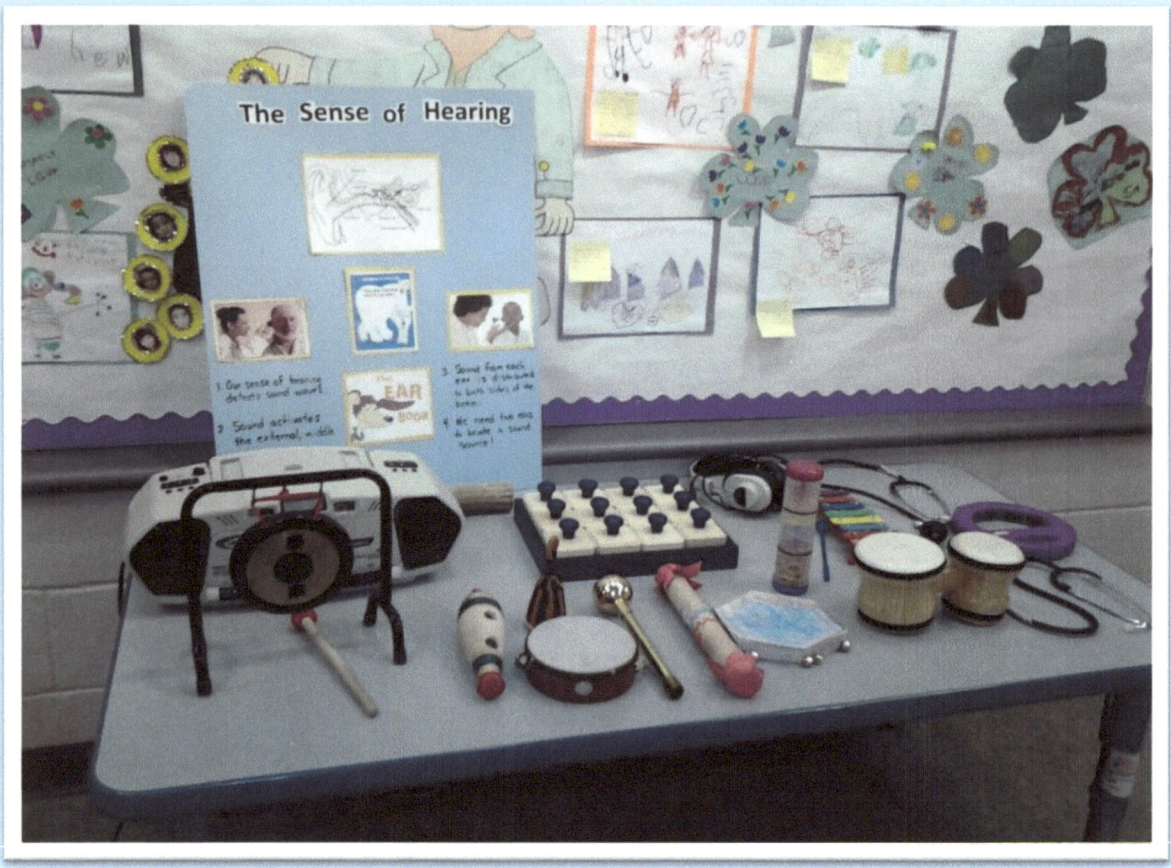

Here is a music display combining hearing and listening posters along with children's work.

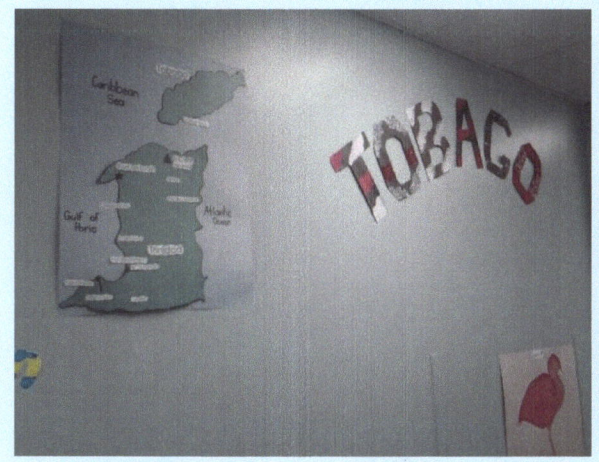

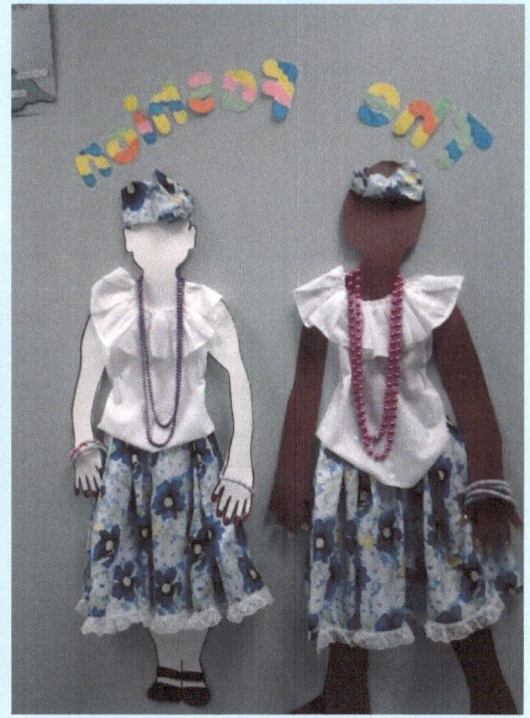

Multicultural display about

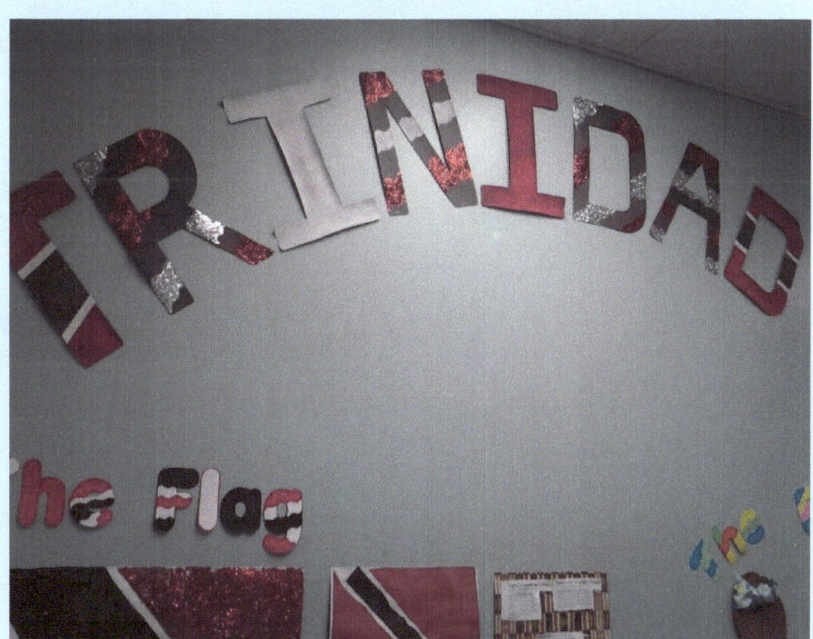

Trinidad.

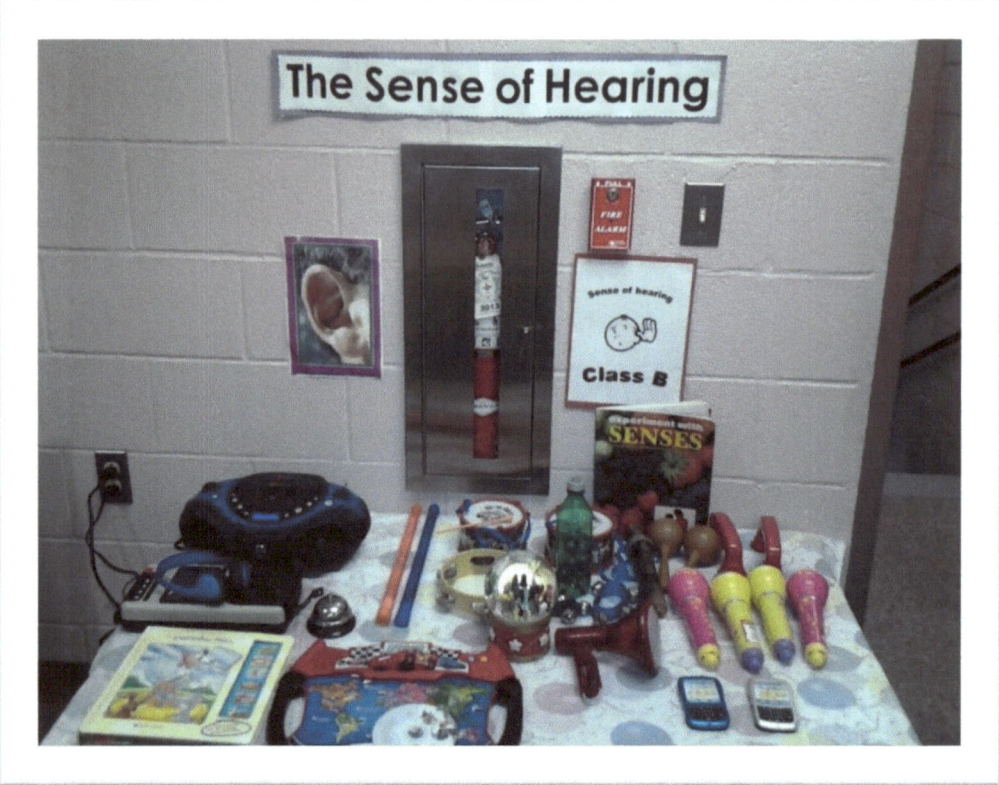

A sense of hearing" interactive display where children explore their hearing.

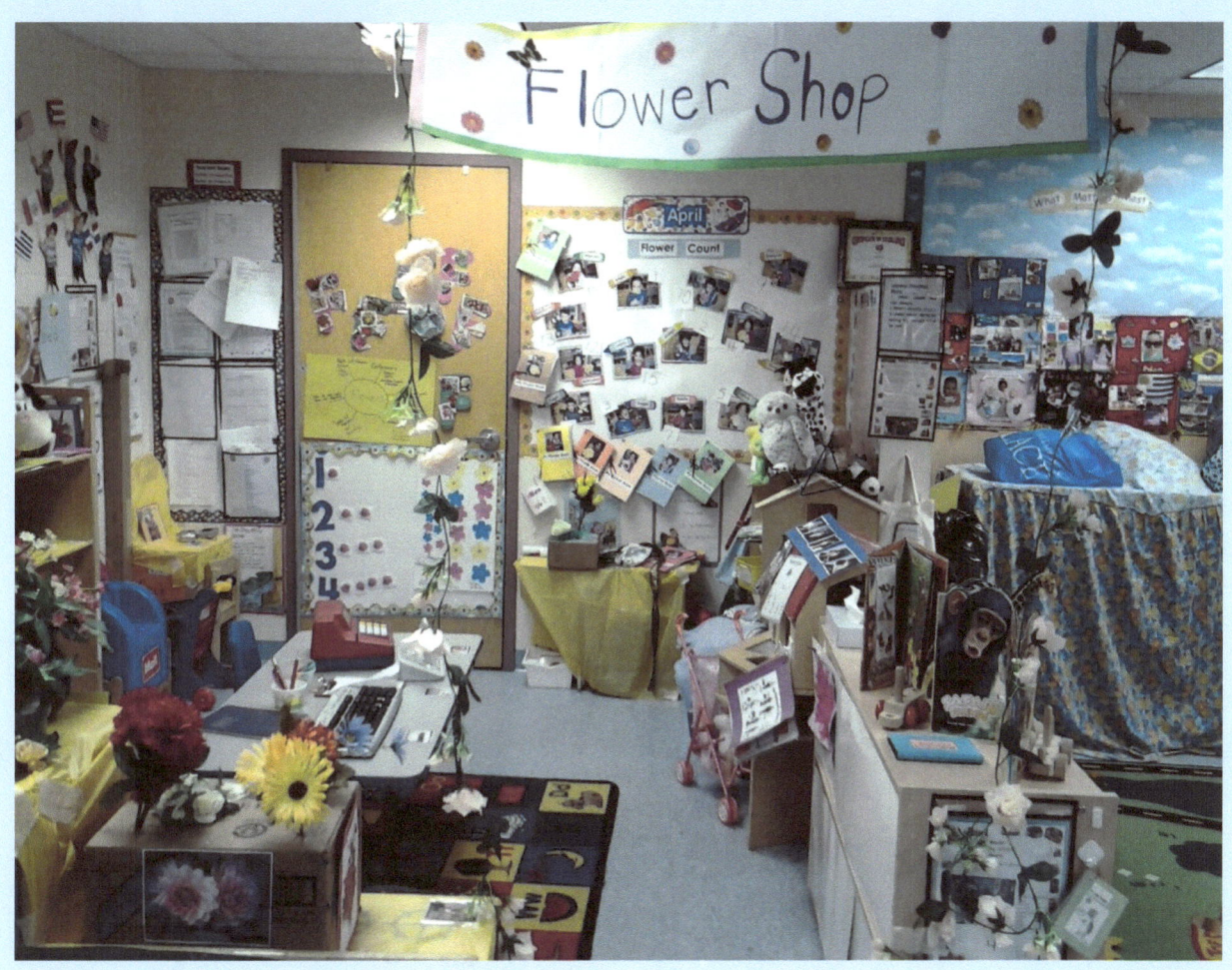

The dramatic play area is transformed into a flower shop.

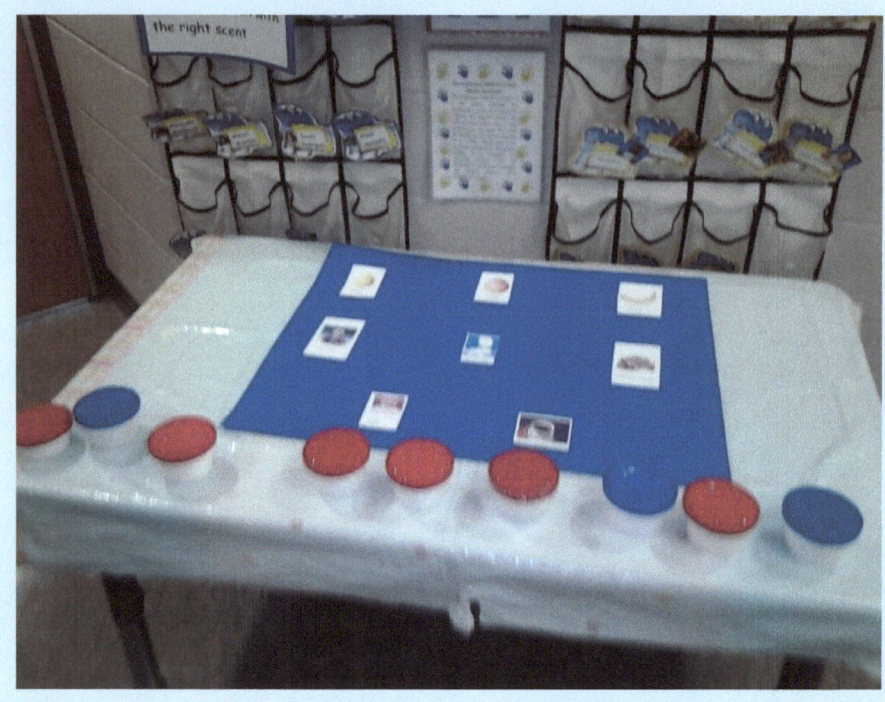

This is an interactive display of various scent containers for preschoolers to smell.

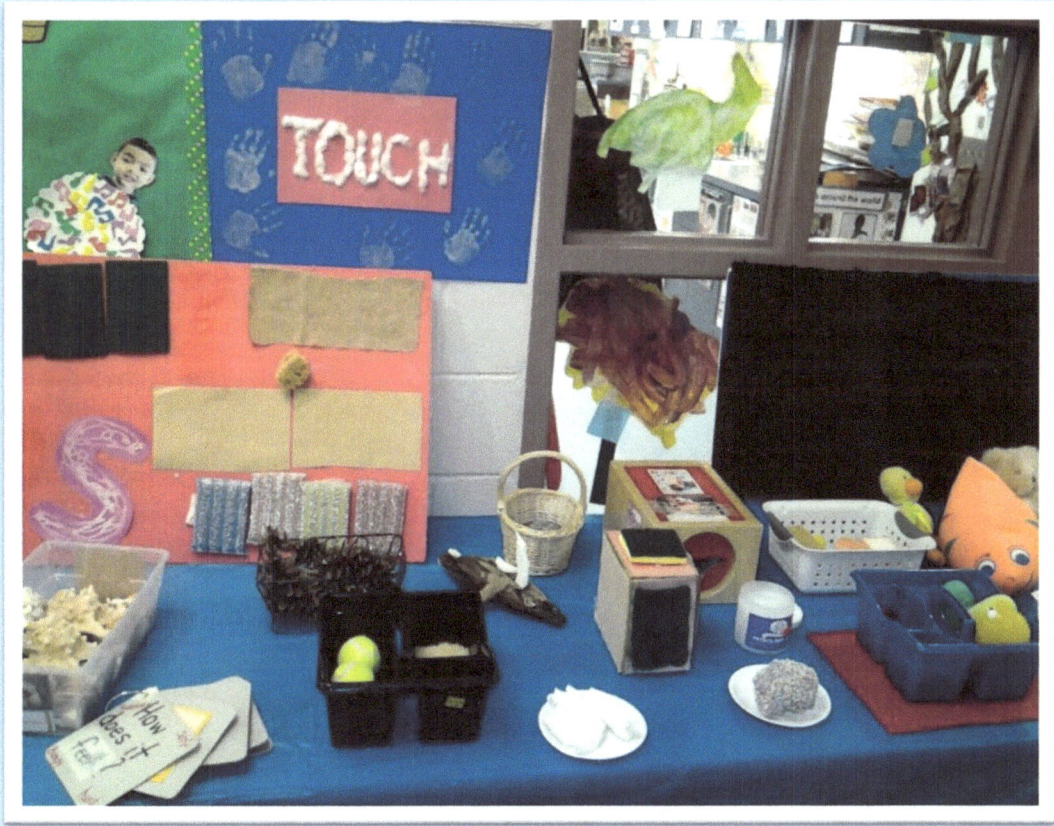

Here is a touch display where preschoolers touch various materials.

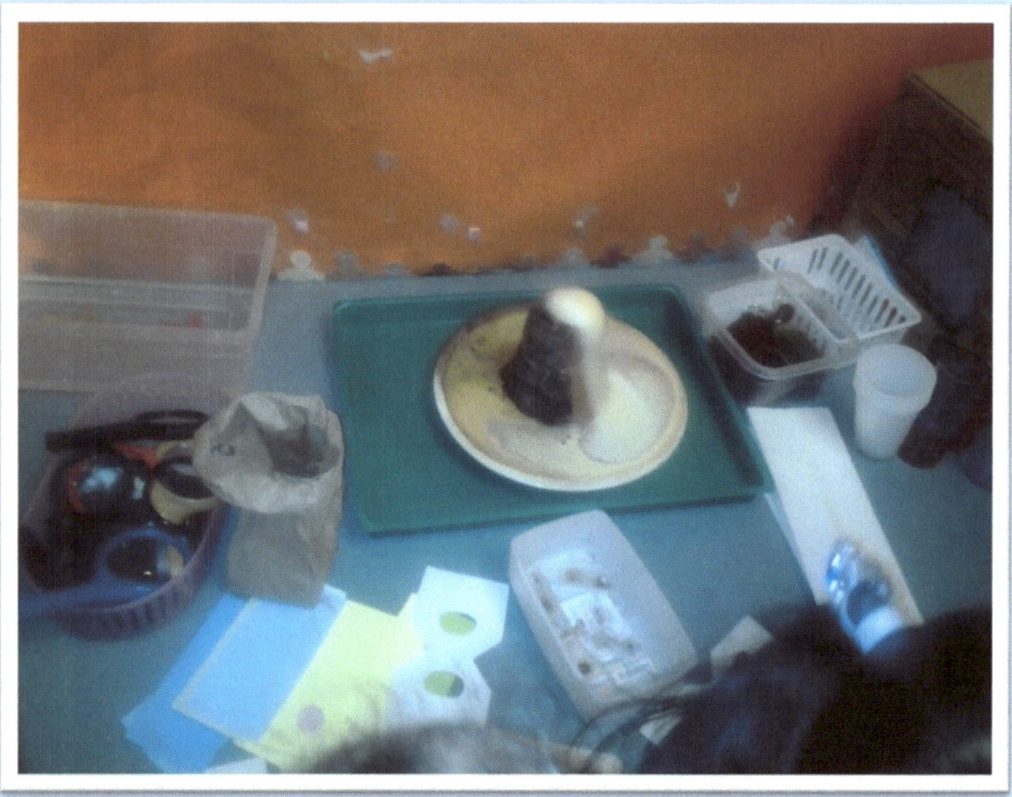

Preschoolers learn how a volcano erupts. Notice the various tools for children to investigate.

A sense of smell

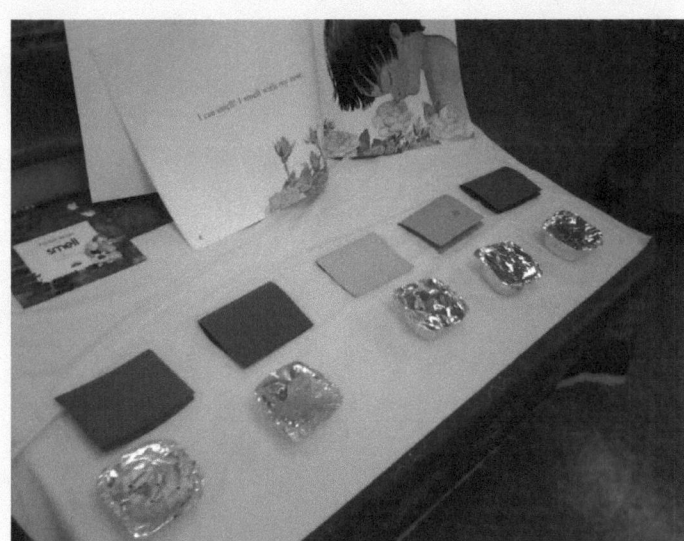

This is a creative way to display
what preschoolers will learn
about the sense of smell.

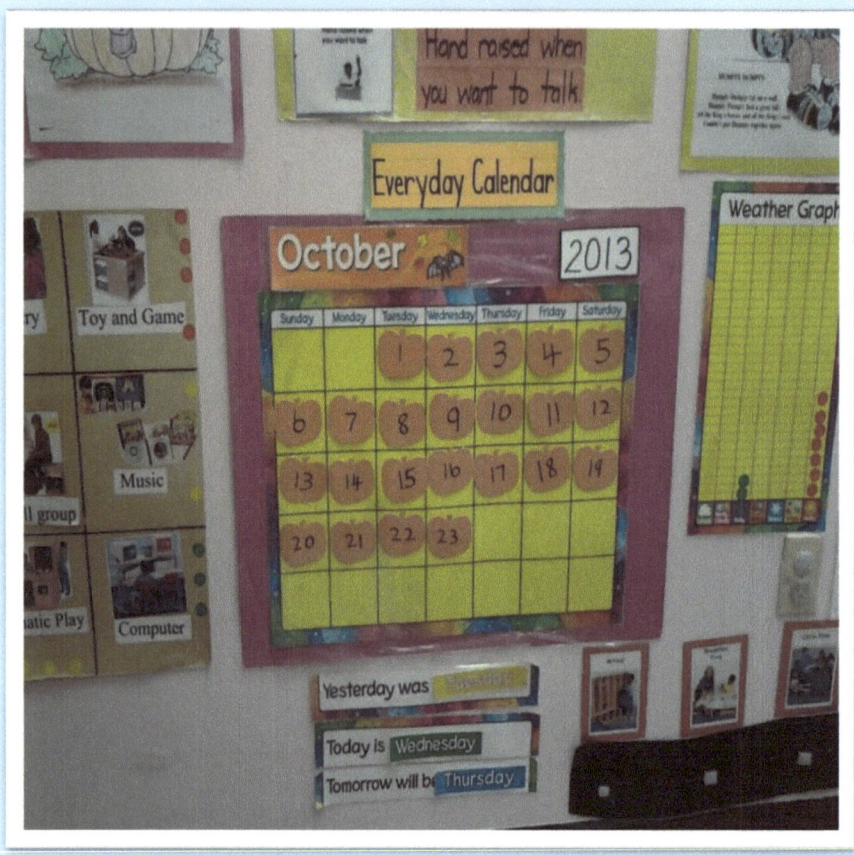

A calendar with pumpkins and numbers—what else could be used to enhance this calendar?

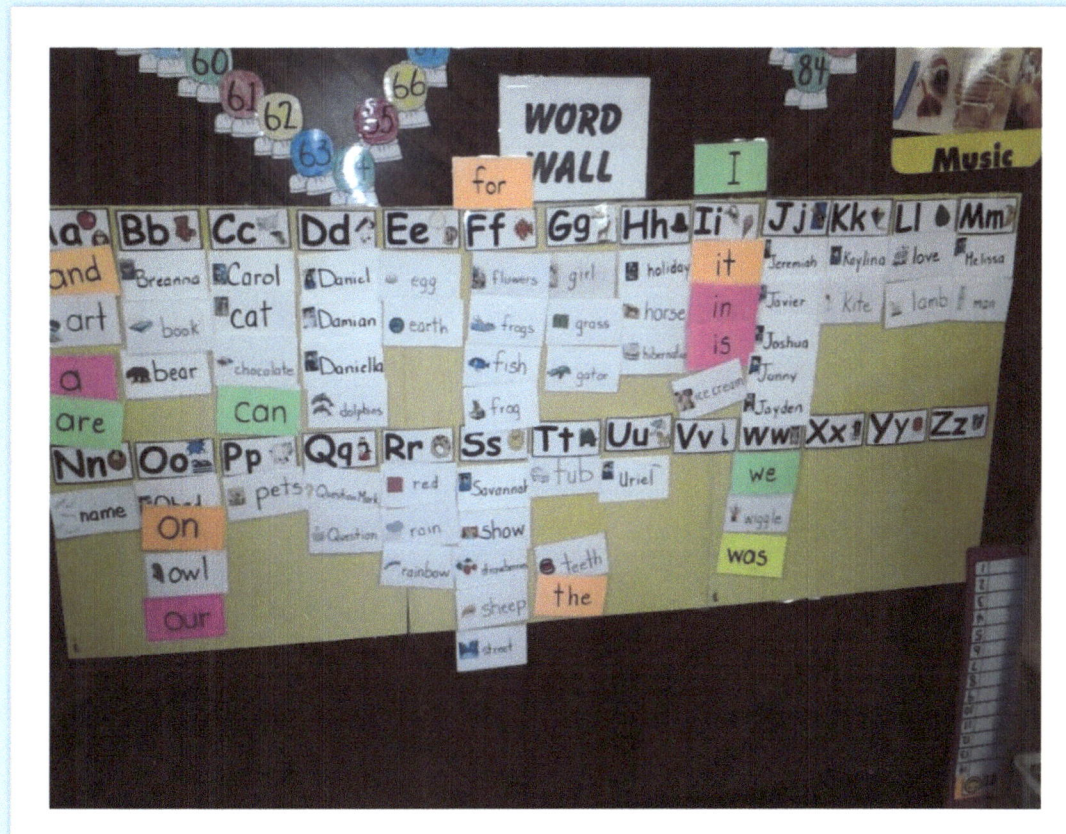

Word wall display

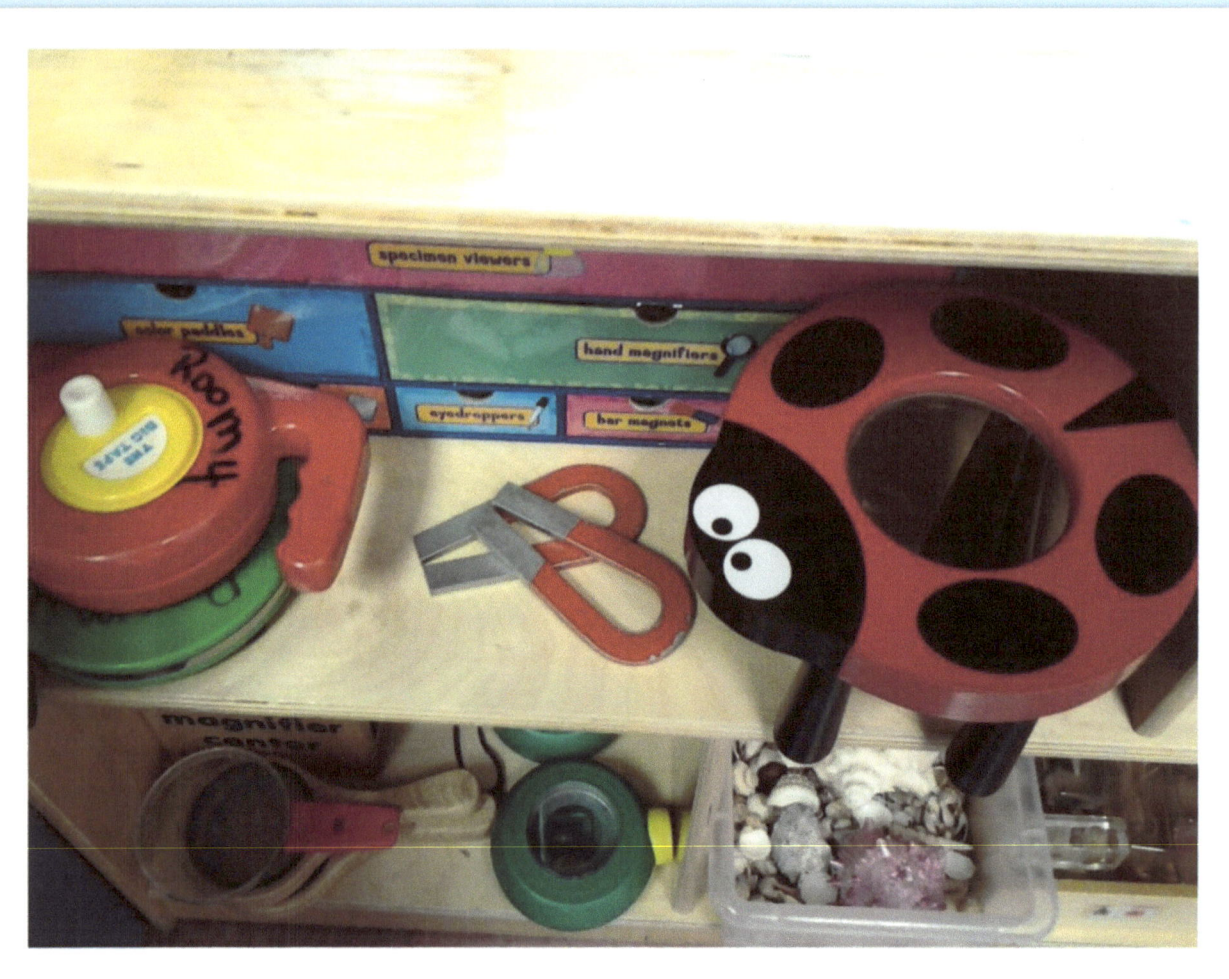

Discovery items on shelves

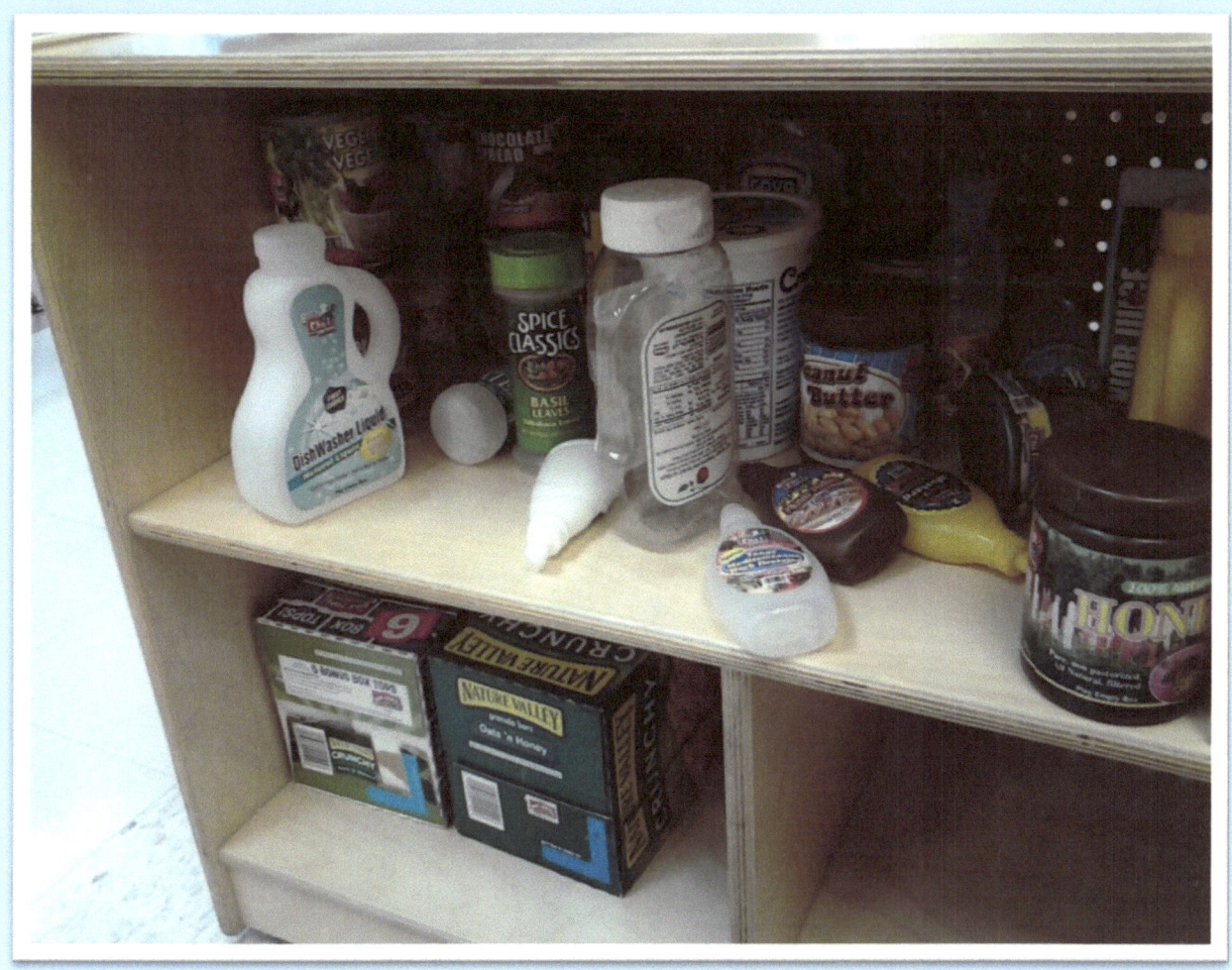

Grocery items for environmental print.

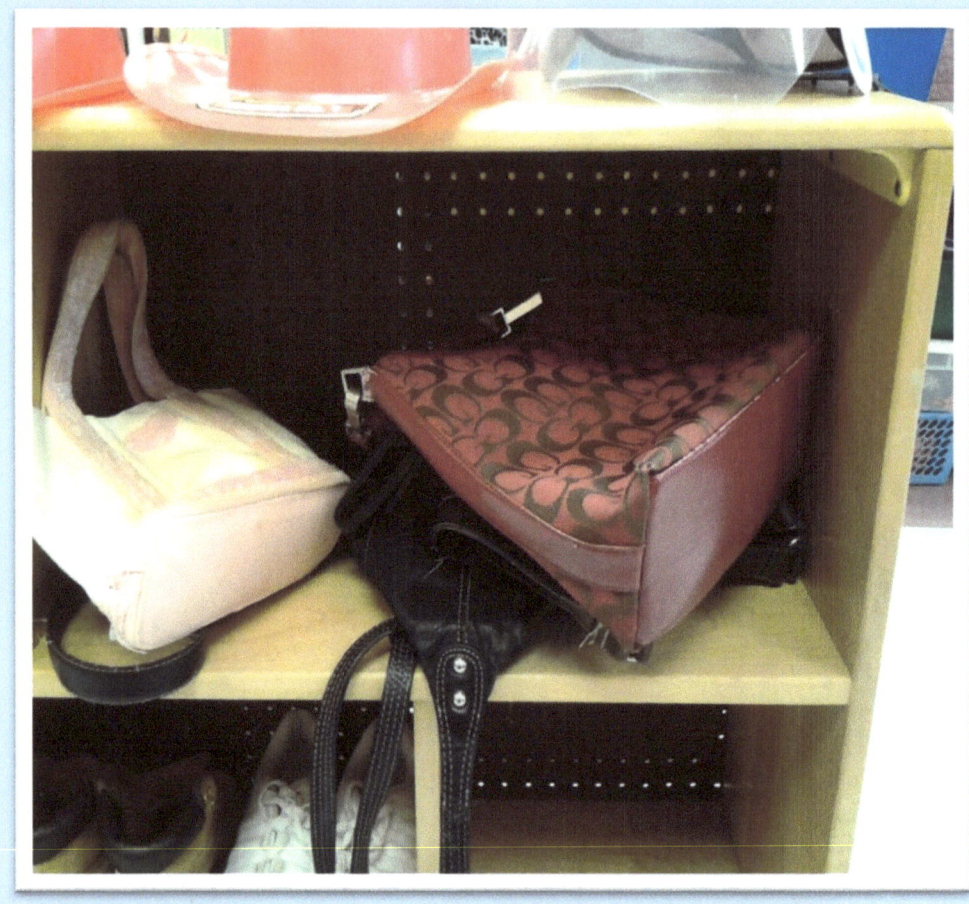

These are handbags and shoes in the dramatic play area. How else can these items be organized?

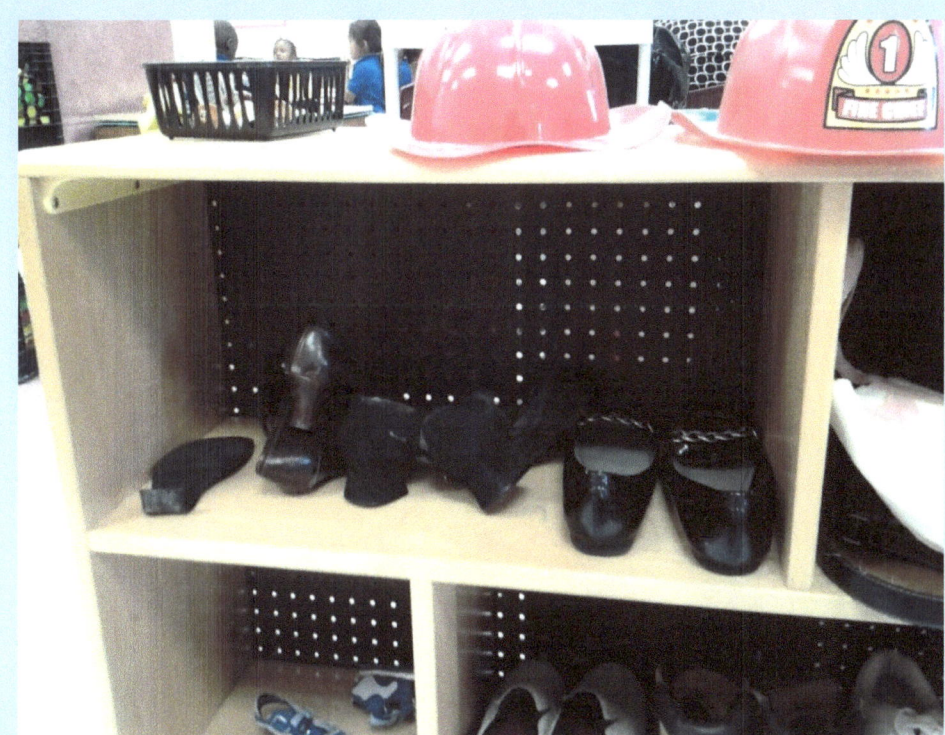

Shoes in the dramatic play area
make sure to label or outline
the shelves with a picture.

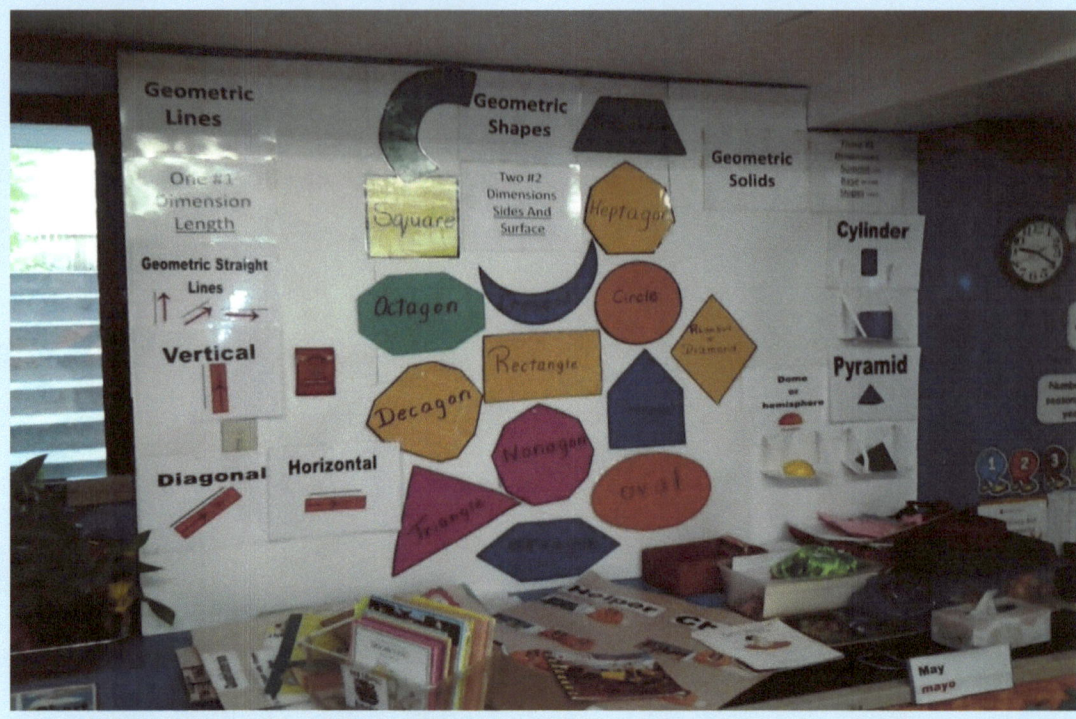

One dimensional shapes
display makes sure to use real
life objects also so children can
handle.

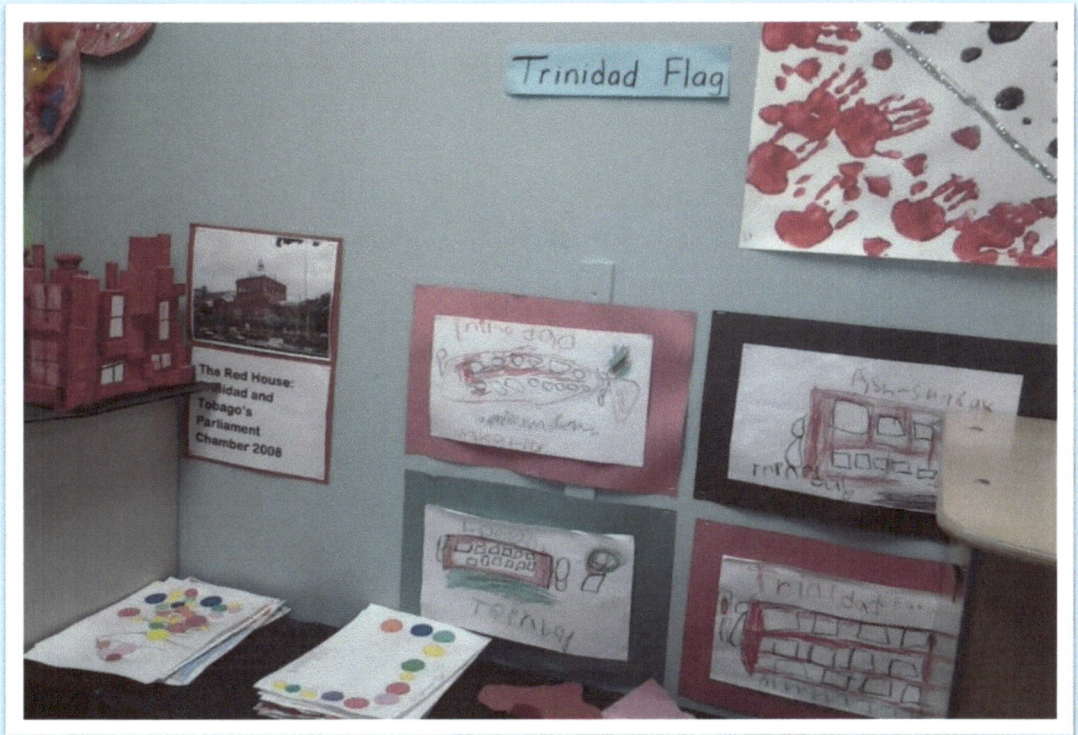

Here is a multicultural display using children's own artwork.

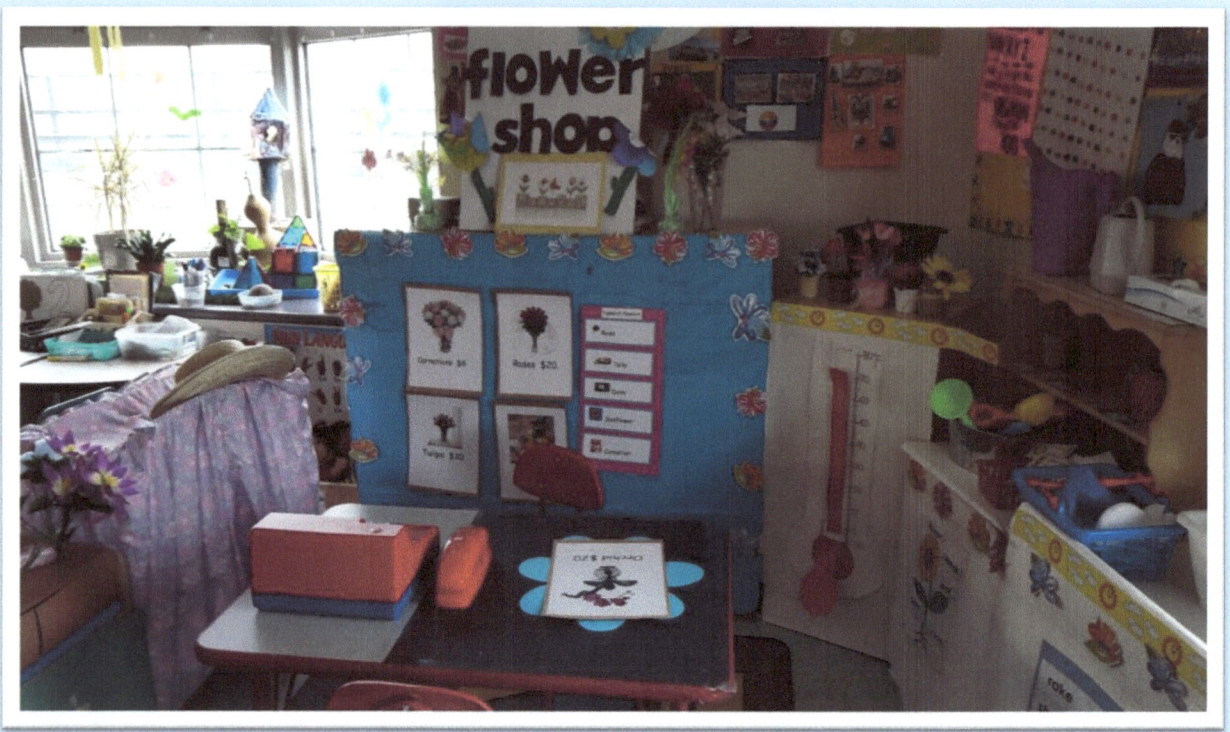

Flower shops in the dramatic play area also notice the thermometer and other items the teacher added.

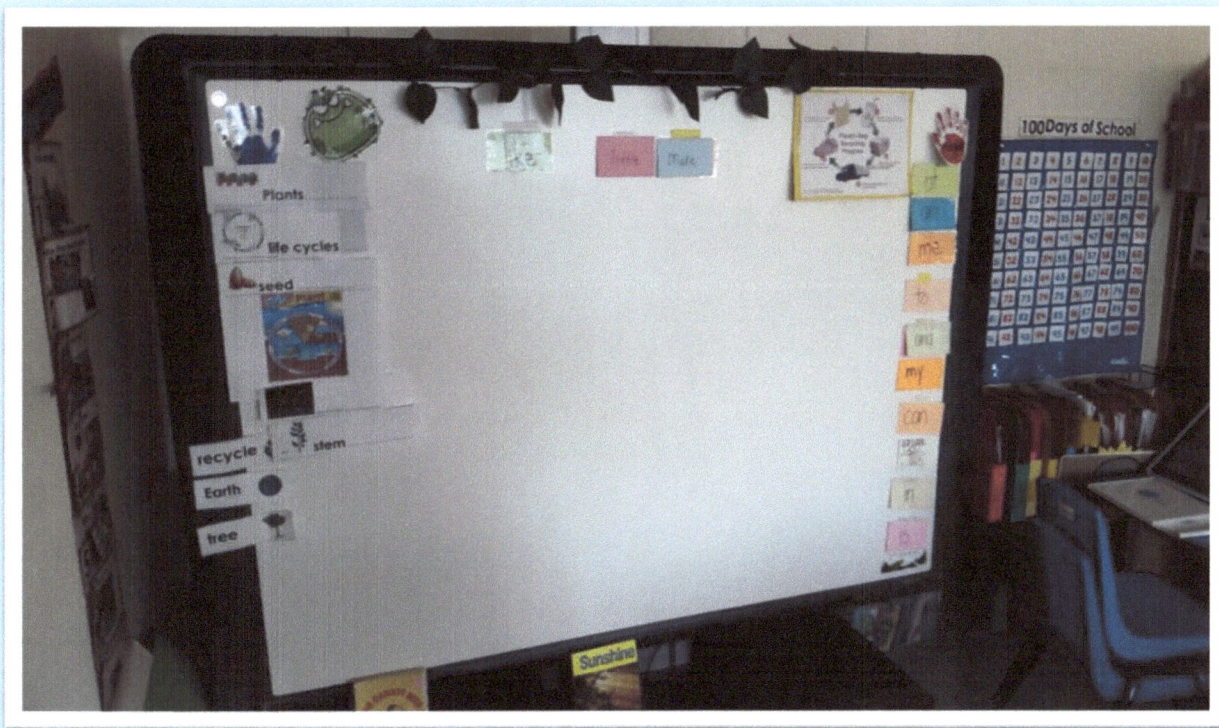

The Smartboard is used to post vocabulary words and high frequency words when there is no wall space.

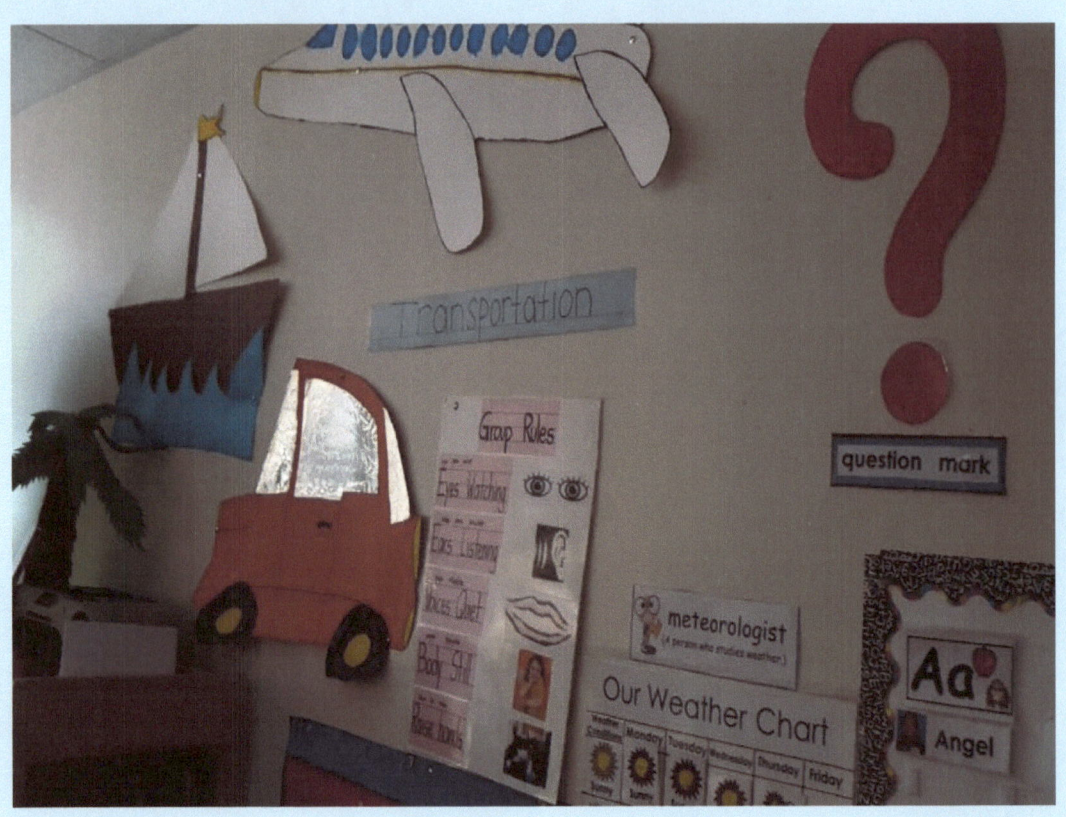

A study relating to the different means of transportation.

Books by Evelyn Ayum

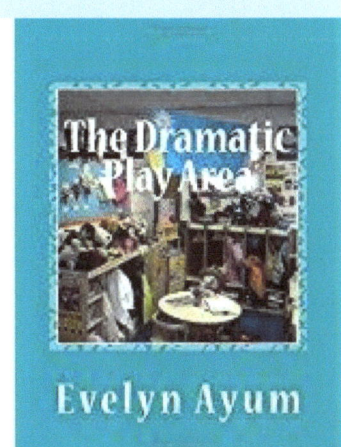

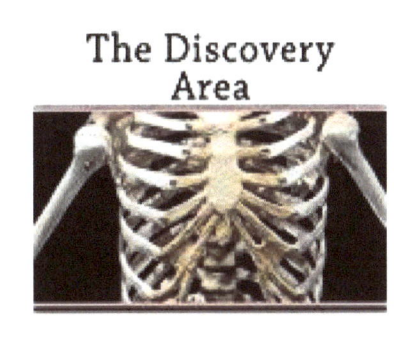

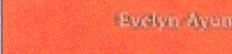

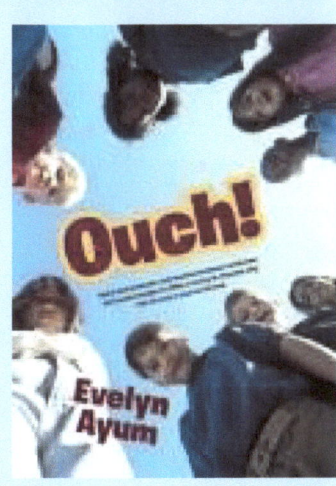

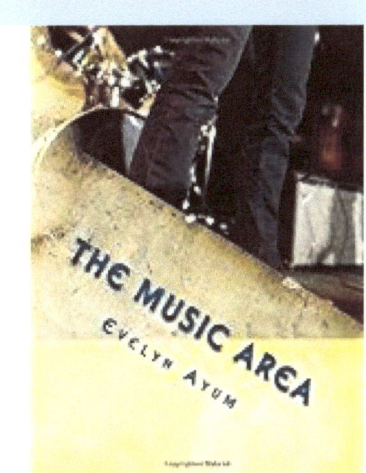

Books by Evelyn Ayum

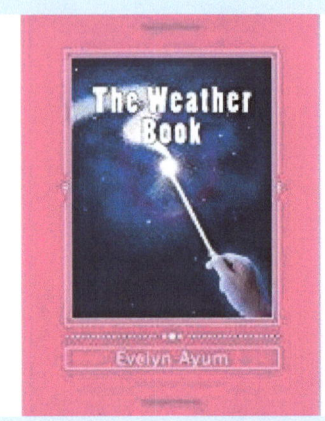

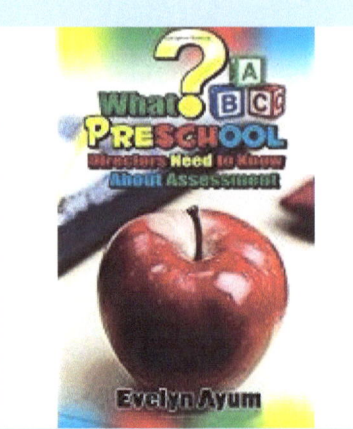

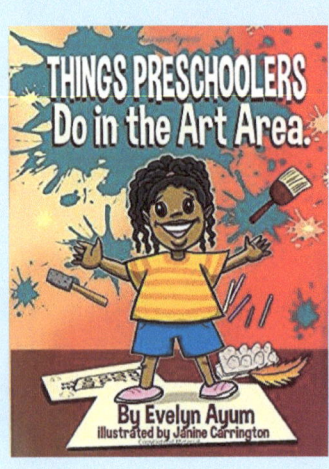

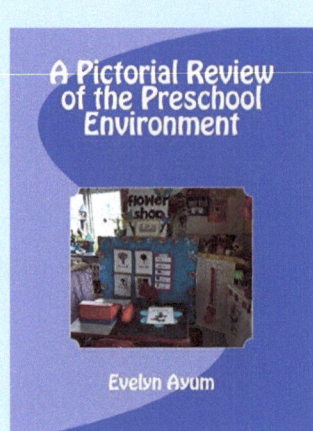

Thanks for your purchase, please provide feedback online, we welcome your reflections. Ebolocs@aol.com. Please note the additions to this book will change over time with other new and creative ideas related to the environment.

Sincerely,

Evelyn Ayum

www.ingramcontent.com/pod-product-compliance
Lightning Source LLC
Chambersburg PA
CBHW050736180526
45159CB00003B/1247